# WHEN GOING WITH THE FLOW ISN'T ENOUGH

... swim upstream

Mary Detweiler

credo
house publishers

Published in the United States by Credo House Publishers, a division of Credo Communications, LLC, Grand Rapids, Michigan
www.credohousepublishers.com

Unless otherwise indicated, all Scripture quotations are taken from the Holy Bible, New Living Translation, copyright © 1996, 2004, 2007, 2013 by Tyndale House Foundation. Used by permission of Tyndale House Publishers, Inc., Carol Stream, Illinois 60188. All rights reserved.

Scripture quotations marked (RSV) are from the Revised Standard Version of the Bible, copyright 1946, 1952 and 1971 National Council of the Churches of Christ in the United States of America. Used by permission. All rights reserved.

ISBN: 978-1-625860-71-2

Cover and interior design by Frank Gutbrod
Editing by Elizabeth Banks

*Printed in the United States of America*

First edition

# Dedication

To all God's daughters. I hope that the words you read in these pages will encourage you to grow into the people God created you to be. "Fan into flames the spiritual gift God gave you . . . . For God has not given us a spirit of fear and timidity, but of power, love, and self-discipline" (2 Timothy 1:6–7). If you find that you have to swim upstream in the process, take heart in the knowledge that you are in good company. Many individuals, both men and women, swam upstream before you. Because they did, they became better people and the world became a better place.

# Table of Contents

# INTRODUCTION

Political and social movements which have changed the course of human history have always been orchestrated by individuals with a clear vision, a consuming passion, the courage to swim upstream against the status quo, the willingness to deal with the consequences of swimming upstream, and the perseverance to keep going no matter what.

As a woman who passionately believes in gender equality and lives in Lancaster County, Pennsylvania, I swim upstream on an almost daily basis. It's tiring and it's isolating. In light of this, then, you might be wondering why in the world I continue to do it. I do it because I have a dream. I have a dream that the following words of Robert Kennedy, the apostle Paul, and Martin Luther King Jr. will finally come true.

- "Some men see things as they are and say why. I dream things that never were and say why not." Robert Kennedy spoke these words repeatedly as he campaigned for the democratic presidential nomination in 1968.

- "There is no longer Jew or Gentile, slave or free, male and female. For you are all one in Christ Jesus" (Galatians 3:28). The apostle Paul wrote these words to the church in Galatia in the first century.

- "I have a dream that my four little children will one day live in a nation where they will not be judged by the color of their skin but by the content of their character." Martin Luther King Jr. proclaimed these words to thousands of people on August 28, 1963, at the Lincoln Memorial in Washington, DC.

My dream is that children, as well as adults, will be able to pursue their dreams regardless of their gender, rather than having roles assigned to them based on their gender. Though I have this dream, I do not have any illusions that I will lead a political or social movement which will result in full gender equality. I also have no illusions that gender equality will become a reality in my lifetime. Rather, I am hoping to plant seeds for change in some hearts.

The perception of women as inferior to men, and the rigid roles women are expected to assume (by both men *and* women) in marriages, families, and churches here in Lancaster County saddens me and angers me. It also saddens me and angers me to know that Lancaster County is far from the only place on the planet where a rigidly patriarchal culture exists. As Jimmy Carter said,

"There is a . . . system of discrimination, extending far beyond a small geographical region to the entire globe; it touches every nation, perpetuating and expanding the trafficking in human slaves, body mutilation, and even legitimized murder on a massive scale. This system is based on the presumption that men and boys are superior to women and girls, and it is supported by some male religious leaders who distort the Holy Bible, the Koran, and other sacred texts to perpetuate their claim that females are, in some basic ways, inferior to them, unqualified to serve God on equal terms. Many men disagree but remain quiet in order to enjoy the benefits of their dominant status. This false premise provides a justification for sexual discrimination in almost every realm of secular and religious life."[1]

Though I understand that gender inequality is global, this book is specifically about gender inequality in the United States, and the role the Christian church has played in maintaining this inequality.

*Important note:* Throughout this book whenever I use the word "church" I am referring to any group of people anywhere who believe in Jesus Christ and who come together regularly to praise and worship him. I am not referring to a building or to any particular congregation or denomination. To highlight this point: if you asked first-century Christians what a church was or why you should go to church, they would not understand the question. Why? Because they *WERE* the church.

*Another important note:* I realize that there are some Christian denominations and congregations that embrace gender equality. These church bodies place individuals in leadership roles based solely on spiritual gifts and calling, not gender. I applaud these churches and appreciate and honor them. I also realize that there are many churches that do not embrace equality. These churches place individuals in roles based on gender, rather than spiritual gifts and calling alone. If you are part of one of these churches, I pray you read this book and let the words you read encourage you to evaluate your position regarding gender roles.

The struggle to achieve gender equality in the United States has many similarities to the struggle to achieve racial equality. As a matter of fact, the two struggles have mirrored and paralleled each other almost from the beginning. Therefore, the stories of these two movements will be intertwined throughout this book.

*One more important note:* I am keenly aware that Native Americans were seen by white settlers as nonpersons and were treated as such. I personally believe the way they were treated was horrific. However, including them as an additional focus is beyond the scope of this book. Though Native Americans will not specifically be addressed and their story will not be told here, please know that I am not insensitive or oblivious to how their lands were stolen from them and their cultures were decimated. Whenever anyone is treated as a nonperson it hurts my heart and angers me.

## Back on Track

Though tremendous legislative strides have been made regarding both racial and gender equality, it is sad but true to acknowledge that racism and sexism still exist. They exist because "isms" are not legal conditions, they are heart conditions and legislation does not change hearts. Civil rights legislation taught us that. I believe that if sexism and racism are to truly come to an end, hearts need to change in a way that leaves people color-blind and gender-blind, seeing each other as equal—different yet equal.

Lasting change begins on the inside—in our hearts. Our thoughts, feelings, attitudes and values change first. *Then* our behavior changes to line up with the internal changes. If our hearts don't change, we may be able to maintain behavioral changes for a while, however, it won't last. We will eventually go back to behaving in a way that reflects our heart. Jesus Christ made this point to a group of Pharisees when he said, "A good person produces good things from the treasury of a good heart, and an evil person produces evil things from the treasury of an evil heart" (Matthew 12:35).

I know that the United States is light years ahead of some other countries in regard to gender equality, and I would like to take this opportunity to express my deep gratitude and appreciation for the strides that have been made in the United States regarding this issue. I would also like to applaud the courage and perseverance of the many men and women who swam upstream to make this happen. Having said that, I also realize that we still have a ways to go in order to achieve full gender equality in the United States. Hearts still need to change, though laws have already changed.

Throughout this book I will be highlighting individuals who made significant contributions to both the civil rights movement and the women's rights movement. I am hoping that their stories will touch your hearts, as well as encourage and inspire you to swim upstream against gender inequality in the church, if you feel moved to do so.

## Change Does Not Come Without a Cost

The gains that have been made regarding both racial equality and gender equality in the world could not have been made without the commitment to act and the willingness to experience the consequences of their actions that each of these individuals made. The same holds true for effecting change in the church. Significant change does not come without a cost.

There is a critical difference, however, between effecting change in the world and effecting change in the church. The difference is this: Fighting for gender equality in the church is not about women's rights or affirmative action. It is about spiritual liberation. It is about truly allowing Christ to be the head of the church by following the leading of the Holy Spirit when choosing who will serve in what ministry roles. It is about allowing individuals with the spiritual gift of leadership to lead, and allowing individuals with the spiritual gift of preaching, to preach, *regardless of their gender*.

## A Call to Act

If you are experiencing discrimination in the church due to your gender, or you see others experiencing discrimination for the same reason, I encourage you to do something to let the discriminators know that what they are doing is not okay. Not everyone will participate in a major political or social movement however, everyone can do something. Helen Keller once said, "I cannot do everything, but I can do something. I will not refuse to do the something I can do."

I am writing this book in the hope that the words you are about to read will light a fire in your heart, making it difficult, if not impossible, for you to stand idly by as long as *any* members of the human race are treated by *anyone* as inferior second-class citizens. I hope you do the something you can do.

# CHAPTER ONE

# BACKSTORY

One of my all-time favorite movies is *The Sound of Music*. When Maria is teaching the von Trapp children to sing she says "Let's start at the very beginning, a very good place to start." So, since this book is focusing on gender inequality in the United States, let's start at the beginning.

As stated in the introduction, political and social movements which have changed the course of human history have always been orchestrated by individuals with a clear vision, a consuming passion, the courage to swim upstream against the status quo, the willingness to deal with the consequences of swimming upstream, and the perseverance to keep going no matter what. The establishment of the United States of America as an independent nation was no exception.

The American Revolution, which was fought from 1775 to 1783, liberated the thirteen American colonies from English rule. George Washington, Alexander Hamilton, John Jay, and James Madison then took the lead in uniting the thirteen independent states into one nation. *The Quartet* by Joseph Ellis tells the story of how they did this. Until

I read *The Quartet* I had no idea how hard and how long these four men had to swim upstream to make this happen.

> The resolution declaring independence, approved on July 2, 1776, clearly states that the former colonies were leaving the British Empire . . . as "Free and Independent States." . . . It was presumed that any faraway national government would represent a domestic version of Parliament, too removed from the interests and experiences of the American citizenry to be trusted. And distrusting such distant sources of political power had become a core ideological impulse of the movement for independence.[2]

Following the approval of the Declaration of Independence, the delegates reconvened to develop a structure which could effectively govern the newly created United States of America. Needless to say, this endeavor involved much debate.

> The debate exposed three fundamental disagreements: first, a sectional split between northern and southern states over slavery; second, a division between large and small states over representation; and third, a more general argument between proponents for a confederation of sovereign states and advocates for a more consolidated national union.[3]

Slavery had already been passionately debated by the delegates to the Continental Congress as they reviewed the document Thomas Jefferson had written declaring the independence of the thirteen American colonies from England. The original draft of the Declaration of Independence included a clause abolishing slavery. This clause sparked fierce debate among the delegates. There is a heart-rending scene of this debate in the movie *1776*. The debate culminates in a volatile confrontation between Thomas Jefferson and John Rutledge of South Carolina in which Rutledge refers to slaves as "property" and Jefferson refers to them as "people being treated as property." Rutledge demands that the clause abolishing slavery be removed from the Declaration of Independence. When Thomas Jefferson and John Adams refuse to remove the clause, all the delegates from the southern colonies walk out of the room.

When the delegates reconvened the next morning to vote on whether or not to accept the resolution for independence, the North Carolina and South Carolina delegations, led by Rutledge, assured Jefferson and Adams that they would vote no if the clause to abolish slavery remained in the document. Since all thirteen colonies needed to vote yes in order for the resolution to pass, Jefferson, with much regret, removed it. "Although most of the prominent founders . . . fully recognized that slavery was incompatible with the values of the American Revolution, they consciously subordinated the moral to the political agenda, permitting the continuance and expansion of slavery as the price to pay for nationhood."[4]

Then, as the delegates were debating what shape the government of the newly created United States would be, they understandably tiptoed around the issue of slavery because they understood that it "possessed the potential to destroy the political consensus that had formed around independence."[5] It was impossible to avoid the issue completely though, as it was such an integral part of the southern economy. It unavoidably came up when they were trying to decide what the tax structure would be to pay expenses associated with the War for Independence. The delegates were in agreement that the cost should be shared by all thirteen states and that each state's portion would be determined by its population or number of inhabitants. The conflict arose when they began to define inhabitants.

The delegates from the southern states insisted that slaves were property and therefore should not be counted. The delegates from the northern states believed that slaves were people and should be counted as inhabitants. "The South Carolina delegation . . . issued the ultimate threat. If the northern states insisted on this point, 'there is an end to the confederation.'"[6]

The delegates resolved this conflict by sidestepping the issue. They decided that a state's payment portion would be determined by the value of its land, rather than the number of its inhabitants.

In November 1777 the delegates finally agreed on a framework of government. They outlined it in the Articles of Confederation and sent it to the states for ratification. This document clearly structured the United States as a confederation of independent states, not one united nation. Approximately one hundred amendments were sent back to the Continental Congress from various states for consideration by the delegates. Most of these proposed amendments were "designed to protect local and state interests from federal encroachment."[7] That's how strong the opposition was to a centralized federal government. The Articles of Confederation was eventually finalized and ratified by all thirteen states in 1781.

The slavery issue came up again in 1783 when the Virginia legislature elected Thomas Jefferson as a delegate to the Confederation Congress, as it was called then. Jefferson was appointed chair of the committee "that would prepare a plan for developing and governing the western lands. The result was the Ordinance of 1784, in all respects save one a thoroughly Jeffersonian document. . . . In order to underline the presumption that the core principles of the American Revolution would prevail in the steady march across the continent, Jefferson insisted that all hereditary titles and privileges would be repudiated and that slavery would end no later than 1800."[8] The ordinance did not pass Congress.

By the end of the War for Independence (1783) George Washington, Alexander Hamilton, John Jay, and James Madison had each, in his own way and in his own time and for his own reasons, come to the conclusion that the framework for government outlined in the Articles of Confederation would not work in postwar America. They all advocated for one united nation. In taking this position they were by far in the minority. The vast majority of influential leaders at that time fervently believed that one nation with a centralized federal government would be a domestic version of the English Parliament and as such could not be trusted to take into account local and regional concerns when governing.

The stream flowing against these four men, therefore, was like a major river after a series of torrential downpours with the riverbanks under water and the current rushing downstream very fast and very powerfully. Swimming upstream against it must have seemed very daunting to them. They didn't let it stop them though, and swim upstream they did.

## Proposals

Alexander Hamilton drafted the first proposal to reform the Articles of Confederation in 1783. The Confederation Congress refused to even debate it. John Jay wanted to take it even further. He advocated for replacing the Articles, not just revising them. "Over the course of the next two years, several proposals calling for a convention to revise the Articles floated through the Congress, one by Madison emphasizing the need for federal control over commerce, another by Charles Pinckney of South Carolina. . . . None of these proposals were as specific or sweeping as Hamilton's, but all met the same fatal fate."[9]

Finally, in January 1786, Congress granted approval for a convention to take place at Annapolis to discuss the rules governing interstate commerce. Delegates from only five states showed up in Annapolis, not enough to proceed. The failure of the remaining state governments to send delegates to the convention was an unmistakably loud nonverbal statement of their opposition to "any federal government that challenged their sovereignty."[10] The residents of the states, for their part, were so busy living their lives they were mostly oblivious to what was occurring politically.

Then, in the fall of 1786, approximately 2000 farmers in western Massachusetts attempted to seize a federal arsenal as an act of protest against mortgage foreclosures and tax increases by the state legislature aimed at retiring the war debt. Jay, Madison, and Hamilton all saw this as "symptomatic of looming anarchy or dissolution of the current confederation into a series of smaller sovereignties."[11] Simultaneously, "within the Confederation Congress there was an emerging sense that reform of the Articles was probably necessary in order to ensure the survival of the confederation."[12] Therefore, planning began to hold a convention in Philadelphia to explore reforming the Articles of Confederation and Congress authorized state legislatures to appoint delegates to this convention.

In the months leading up to the convention, Madison corresponded with the men who would be the most influential delegates. In his letters to them he presented his position that the only acceptable outcome of the convention would be a government structured in a way that shifted sovereignty from the state to the national level. He built his case point by point like a master attorney. He then outlined a system of government which eventually became the skeletal system for our current Constitution.

In addition, he engaged in meticulous preparation for the convention, reading everything he could get his hands on "about the historical fate of confederacies and the challenges faced by previous efforts to establish a republican form of government on a national scale.... His reading was driven by a clear sense of the arguments he anticipated from confederationists and the arguments he needed to make for a nation-size republic."[13]

The convention finally convened in mid-May 1787 and elected George Washington to be the chair. They met in the same room where the Declaration of Independence had been debated and signed.

> By choosing the same city, the same building, even the same room where those values were first discovered and declared, the delegates were making a statement—whether they knew it or not—that whatever they produced should be regarded as a continuation rather than a rejection of "the spirit of '76." This made the convention a new chapter in a continuing story—not a break with the past but an expression of its full meaning. And no less a figure than Washington himself seemed to be nodding in agreement with this story line as he sat in that high-backed wooden chair.[14]

Madison's meticulous preparation paid off on May 30 "when a majority of delegates endorsed the resolution ... 'for a national government ... consisting of a supreme legislature, executive, and judiciary.'"[15] Over the ensuing months "an ever-shifting collection of delegates from twelve states met in general sessions, on appointed committees, and in informal gatherings."[16]

## Pink Elephants

There were two pink elephants in the room throughout the Constitutional Convention (as it came to be called) which the delegates tiptoed around, refusing to even name them out loud. The first one was monarchy and the second one was slavery.

Regarding monarchy:

> Any robust expression of executive power was forced to fight a constant rearguard action against accusations of monarchy. . . . The debate over the executive took up more time and energy than any other issue at the convention, largely because the delegates could not agree on how much authority to place in the office; whether it should be a single person or a troika representing the northern, middle, and southern states; how long he should serve (a woman was unimaginable); and how he should be elected and impeached.[17]

Regarding slavery: Just as in the Continental Congress, slavery was such an explosive and divisive issue that it could have ground the entire convention to a complete halt if directly confronted and debated. Therefore, the delegates did what they had done at previous conventions, they sidestepped the issue.

> A sectional split was, from the beginning, built into the very structure of the convention, and some kind of political compromise was

inevitable if the Constitution were to stand any chance of passage and ratification. . . . The two most explicit decisions implicitly endorsing slavery were the agreement to count slaves as three-fifths of a person for purposes of representation in the House and a prohibition against ending the slave trade for twenty years, concessions to the Deep South, especially South Carolina, that appear horrific to our eyes but without which the Constitution almost certainly could never have come into existence.[18]

Governeur Morris of Pennsylvania is the man who actually wrote the United States Constitution. He took twenty-three articles and condensed them into seven, outlining the political structure which would implement the principles put forth in the Declaration of Independence. The most important change he made was to the preamble. He changed "We the People of the States of . . . (a listing of each state individually)" to "We the people of the United States." The significance of this change cannot be understated. In doing this, he made it clear "that the newly created government operated directly on the whole American citizenry, not indirectly through the States."[19] "We the people," however, really meant "we the men," specifically "we the white men."

The Constitutional Convention came to a close with the signing of the Constitution by thirty-nine delegates on September 17, 1787. The Constitution was then sent to the states to be reviewed and debated in state ratifying conventions. By July 1788 eleven states had ratified the Constitution. The new government was implemented on March 4, 1789.

Though Madison, Hamilton, Jay, and Washington did not accomplish all they had set out to do, they can certainly be applauded for the fact that the Constitutional Convention even happened. If they had not continued to swim upstream against a tidal wave of popular opinion, it never would have occurred. Though they were forced to make some significant compromises (ones they did not want to make), they certainly did change the course of American history. The compromises they and the other nationalists made were inevitable due to the climate of the times, just like the compromises Adams and Jefferson were forced to make in order to have the Continental Congress approve the resolution for independence. Sometimes it really is necessary to lose a battle in order to win a war.

## One Sad Fact

One fact that saddens me greatly, though, is that though slavery was hotly debated, or consciously sidestepped, throughout the processes of declaring independence and framing a government, the issue of the status of women was not on any of the Founding Fathers' radar screens. Regardless of what side of the slavery issue each of the Founding Fathers placed themselves, they all knew it was an issue. This was not true regarding the status of women. It never entered their minds that there was something wrong or problematic with the perceived inferiority of women. The fact that they did not even consider the second-class status of women to be an issue is indicative of how deeply rooted and ingrained this belief was in each of them.

It is interesting to note however, that though none of the Founding Fathers gave any thought at all to the status of women, to say nothing of considering it a problem, the wives of two of the founding fathers did. Both John Adam's wife, Abigail, and James Madison's wife, Dolly, thought there was something wrong with the way women were perceived and treated. "Abigail Adams once predicted that if any of the Framers [of the Constitution] left women out of the new republic they were founding, the 'ladies' would 'foment a rebellion.'"[20] In some correspondence of Dolly Madison's that was recovered later, it was found that in some of her letters she referred to the status of women as similar to the status of slaves.

The reality of two eighteenth-century women thinking along these lines is truly amazing in light of the culture of the time. Their thoughts and written words can be seen as little-known precursors to the women's rights movement.

# CHAPTER TWO

# THE REST OF THE STORY

Paul Harvey was a radio broadcaster for the ABC Radio Networks. He was particularly known for his *Rest of the Story* segments. He started doing these segments as part of his newscasts during the Second World War. The *Rest of the Story* eventually morphed into its own show which premiered in 1976. The format of the show was as follows: Harvey would tell an obscure story leaving out an important detail, usually the name of some well-known person. He would fill in the missing detail at the end, closing with some variation of the tag line "And now you know the rest of the story." The show ran until Harvey's death in 2009.

Though sometimes it's necessary to lose a battle in order to win a war, at other times it's necessary to fight a battle or even a war for no other reason than it needs to be fought. It is important to remember that when an issue is buried in order to achieve a larger purpose, that issue does not go away, particularly such a volatile issue as slavery.

## Buried, but Not Forgotten

Though the issue of slavery had been sidestepped at several strategic points in our early history, it didn't disappear. It simmered just under the surface for decades until it finally boiled over in Kansas in the middle of the next century. The issue of slavery then had to be faced head on and dealt with. Sidestepping it was no longer an option.

The issue of slavery was front and center in the process of the Kansas Territory becoming a state in the mid-1800s. The central question in that process was whether Kansas would enter the Union as a slave state or as a free state. As the process of statehood moved along, Kansas became a battleground between antislavery forces from the North and proslavery forces from the South.

In October 1855, Ohio abolitionist John Brown went to the Kansas Territory to fight against slavery. He led small groups of volunteers in armed skirmishes against proslavery men. Unlike most abolitionists who advocated for peaceful resistance to the proslavery faction, Brown believed that peaceful resistance had proven itself to be ineffective. He believed armed insurrection was the only way to overthrow the institution of slavery in the United States.

In August 1856, thousands of proslavery men formed into armies and marched into Kansas. Violence then enveloped the Kansas territory for the next two months until Brown left Kansas.

Brown and his men then went to Harper's Ferry, Virginia, where they began planning a full-scale slave insurrection. On October 16, 1859, John Brown led a group of twenty-one men in a raid on the federal armory at Harper's Ferry. His intention was to arm slaves with the weapons he planned to steal. He was unsuccessful though, as the raid failed.

Immediately upon the men entering the armory, shots were fired. This alerted the townspeople to what was going on. The townspeople armed themselves and surrounded the building. Brown and his men then barricaded themselves inside, taking some of the townspeople hostage. Within thirty-six hours it was over. Brown's men had fled or been killed or captured by local proslavery farmers, militiamen, and US Marines. John Brown was captured and tried for treason against the Commonwealth of Virginia, for murder, and for inciting a slave insurrection. He was found guilty of all charges and hung on December 2, 1859.

The violence in Kansas and the raid on the Harper's Ferry Armory were undoubtedly catalysts for the Civil War. The election of Abraham Lincoln, who was known to be antislavery, to the presidency in 1860 was the final spark which lit the fire that would not go out until the issue of slavery was settled. The question of whether slaves were people or property needed to be answered once and for all.

After Lincoln was elected and before he was inaugurated, South Carolina seceded from the Union, finally acting on the secessionist threat it had first made at the Continental Congress in 1776. Six other slave-holding states followed South Carolina's lead, also seceding from the Union. They formed the Confederate Nation, and the Civil War erupted soon after this.

The Civil War was fought from 1861 to 1865 and resulted in the abolition of slavery and in the United States remaining one nation. The price that was paid to abolish slavery and keep the nation united was approximately 750,000 soldier deaths. Of those 750,000 soldier deaths, 56,000 died in prisons. Another 60,000 men lost limbs.

In spite of the overwhelming cost that was paid, the abolition of slavery did not result in black people being able to actually exercise their political freedom and civil rights. Many, many more people had to swim upstream and pay huge prices, including the ultimate sacrifice, to make that happen.

## The Beginning of Another Movement

While the nation as a whole was focused on racial equality (either for or against) during the mid-1800s, a few women were getting stirred up about gender equality and were beginning to plant seeds for that movement.

In 1848 Elizabeth Stanton emerged as a women's rights leader. She, along with a handful of other women, organized the Seneca Falls Convention which was held that year in Seneca Falls, New York. Over three hundred people attended. Prior to the convention, Elizabeth wrote a Declaration of Sentiments, which she modeled on the Declaration of Independence. In that document she stated that men and women are created equal and proposed, among other things, a resolution demanding voting rights for women. She read her declaration at the convention. The final resolutions, including female suffrage, were passed. She was then invited to speak at a second women's rights convention in Rochester, New York, solidifying her role as an activist and reformer.

In addition to voting rights for women, Elizabeth's Declaration of Sentiments proposed gender-neutral divorce laws, a woman's right to refuse her husband sexually, increased economic opportunities for women, and the right of women to serve on juries. Elizabeth Stanton was most definitely ahead of her time in her thinking.

In 1851 Elizabeth Stanton met another women's rights leader, Susan B. Anthony. The two women formed a powerful partnership, contributing much to laying a firm foundation for the women's movement. Their skills and their situations complemented each other. Elizabeth was a visionary and a writer. Susan was an organizer and a tactician. Elizabeth was married with seven children. Susan was single. During the years that Elizabeth was home raising her children, she provided the ideas and wrote the speeches. Susan traveled, rented the halls, delivered the speeches, and circulated petitions. For most of her life, Susan lived almost entirely on fees she earned as a speaker.

In 1872, Susan was arrested for voting in her hometown of Rochester, New York. She was convicted in a widely publicized trial and ordered to pay a fine. Though she refused to pay the fine, the authorities did not pursue further legal action.

Susan and Elizabeth then developed a constitutional amendment giving women the right to vote. Aaron A. Sargent (R-CA) introduced it to Congress in January 1878. It did not pass. For the next forty years it was brought before Congress every year, and every year it failed to pass. It finally passed in 1920, becoming the Nineteenth Amendment to the US Constitution giving *white* women the right to vote.

During the forty-year period that this bill was unsuccessfully brought before Congress annually, women suffragists continued to be very active. They did not passively sit back waiting to see if this bill would become law. They promoted swimming competitions, scaled mountains, piloted airplanes and staged large-scale parades to gain publicity. In 1912, they organized a twelve-day, 170-mile "Hike to Albany." In 1913, the suffragist "Army of the Hudson" marched 225 miles from Newark to Washington in sixteen days, with numerous photo and press opportunities along the way. This gained them a national audience. In 1917, they formed The National Woman's Party, an organization that fought for women's right to vote on the same terms as men by lobbying for passage of the constitutional amendment giving women the right to vote.

## The Opposition

Opposition to the women's suffrage movement came from:

- the National Organization Against Women's Suffrage, which was *led by women*;

- southern white men who were afraid that black women would vote;

- ethnic politicians (especially Catholics whose women were not allowed a political voice); and

- drinking men who were afraid (rightfully as it turned out) that women would use their right to vote to enact prohibition of alcoholic beverages.

Opposition to black women's suffrage came from white suffragists. As the movement gained support, white suffragists realized they could gain even more support if they excluded black women. They then began to marginalize as many black women as possible. One way they did this was by promoting the concept of the "educated suffragist"— i.e., the idea that one needed to be educated in order to be allowed to vote. Since primarily only white women were educated, this effectively shut black women out of the suffragist movement. Though this "educated suffragist" movement initially was primarily prevalent in the South, it eventually gained momentum in the North as well. Black women, therefore, not only had to deal with the sexism of being denied the right to vote, they also had to deal with the racism of white suffragists.

## The Final Push

World War I provided the final push for women's suffrage in America. Women were outraged when President Woodrow Wilson announced that World War I was a war for democracy. The National Women's Party picketed outside the White House and engaged in a series of protests against the Wilson Administration in Washington, DC. Wilson ignored the protests for six months, but on June 20, 1917, as a Russian delegation drove up to the White House, suffragettes unfurled a banner which stated "We women of America tell you that America is not a democracy. Twenty million women are denied the right to vote." Another banner on August 14, 1917, referred to "Kaiser Wilson" and compared the plight of the German people with that of American women. As a result

# CHAPTER THREE

# ROCKING THE BOAT

Another favorite movie of mine is *An American President*. There is a scene in that movie in which Martin Sheen's character vehemently states, "You don't fight the fights you can win, you fight the fights that need fighting!"

When President Lincoln issued the Emancipation Proclamation in 1863, slaves in the Confederate States (numbering almost four million people) were set free. The Emancipation Proclamation, however, was issued as a war measure under the president's constitutional authority as commander in chief of the armed forces. As such, it applied only to the states which had rebelled against the Union. It was not a law passed by Congress. To ensure the abolition of slavery in the United States as a whole, Lincoln pushed for passage of the Thirteenth Amendment to the Constitution which stated, "Neither slavery nor involuntary servitude, except as a punishment for crime whereof the party shall have been duly convicted, shall exist within the United States, or any place subject to their jurisdiction." It became law on December 6, 1865.

As is evident from the wording of the Thirteenth Amendment, though slaves were legally set free, they were not guaranteed political and civil rights. Additional legislation was needed for that. In 1865, Congress passed what would become the Civil Rights Act of 1866, guaranteeing citizenship without regard to race, color, or previous condition of slavery or involuntary servitude. This bill also guaranteed equal benefits and access to the law. Then, in 1868, the Fourteenth Amendment to the Constitution was adopted. This amendment granted citizenship to "all persons born or naturalized in the United States," which included former slaves recently freed. In addition, it forbid states from denying any person "life, liberty or property, without due process of law" or to "deny to any person within its jurisdiction the equal protection of the laws." It still did not however, guarantee black citizens the ability to exercise their political and civil rights. Still more legislation was needed for that.

In 1870 Congress adopted the Fifteenth Amendment to the Constitution which prohibits federal and state governments from denying *men* the right to vote due to "race, color, or previous condition of servitude." It did not however, challenge the authority of states and localities to establish and administer their own voting requirements, and many southern states did exactly that. They used various methods such as literacy tests, poll taxes, intimidation, threats, and even violence to keep people of color from voting. White people who could not pass the literacy tests or pay the poll taxes were allowed to vote under grandfather clauses. In addition to discriminatory practices at the polls, local and state laws known as Jim Crow laws banned blacks from schools, public restrooms, lunch counters, theaters, trains, etc.

The struggle for racial equality, also known as the civil rights movement, came to the fore again in the 1950s when a number of individuals began to swim upstream.

It is important to remember that, when an individual or group of individuals swim upstream against the current, any boats that are on the water will rock. These boats will then inevitably, and usually immediately, resist the movement of the swimmer or swimmers in an effort to keep the stream flowing the way it had been flowing—to maintain the status quo. They can then impose consequences on the swimmer or swimmers which can range from the fairly benign to the catastrophic, and this is exactly what happened to civil rights workers.

## The Civil Rights Movement

The goal of the civil rights movement was integration of public facilities and removal of the obstacles put in place to stop black men from voting. Black *women* still were not able to vote.

Civil rights workers achieved their goals through civil disobedience (direct action through nonviolent resistance). Acts of civil disobedience occurred all over the South during the 1950's and 1960's. Many acts of civil disobedience resulted in violent episodes due to law enforcement officers (many of whom were members of the Ku Klux Klan) routinely using night sticks, attack dogs, city fire hoses, billy clubs, and tear gas to force nonviolent, unarmed protesters into submission. This resulted in the deaths of countless southern black men, women, and children. In addition, northerners who traveled to the south to help blacks register to vote were murdered by segregationists. White supremacists also bombed black schools, churches, businesses, and residences.

Through courageous and consistent acts of nonviolent protest, civil rights workers were able to influence legislators to pass the Civil Rights Act of 1964 which outlawed discrimination based on race, color, religion, sex, or national origin. It also prohibited racial segregation in schools, at the workplace and by facilities that served the general public.

## Freedom Riders

One group of civil rights workers I would like to highlight are the Freedom Riders. They rocked *lots* of boats. Freedom Riders were interracial groups of people from the North who boarded buses heading for the South. They rode the buses to challenge the non-enforcement of Supreme Court decisions made in 1946 and 1960, which ruled that segregated interstate buses were unconstitutional as well as segregated restaurants and waiting rooms in bus terminals that served interstate buses. Southern states had ignored these rulings and the federal government had done nothing to enforce them. In 1955, the Interstate Commerce Commission (ICC) denounced the separate but equal doctrine regarding interstate bus travel. The ICC did not enforce this however, and local Jim Crow laws regarding buses and bus terminals remained in effect throughout the South.

The first Freedom Ride left Washington, DC, on May 4, 1961. Over the next six months more than sixty Freedom Rides rolled through the South. It is estimated that approximately 450 riders participated in one or more Freedom Rides. About 75 percent of the riders were males under the age of thirty, with about equal percentages of blacks and whites.

Most of the Freedom Rides were organized and sponsored by either the Congress of Racial Equality (CORE) or the Student Nonviolent Coordinating Committee (SNCC). The Freedom Riders' tactics were to have at least one interracial pair sitting in adjoining seats, and at least one black rider sitting up front, where seats under segregation had been reserved for white customers only by local custom throughout the South. The rest of the team would sit scattered throughout the bus. One rider would abide by the South's segregation rules in order to avoid arrest. It was this rider's responsibility to contact CORE to arrange bail for those who were arrested.

At rest stops, whites would go into black only areas and blacks would go into white only areas. The tactic of black and white Freedom Riders sitting together in segregated restaurants, lunch counters and hotels was especially effective when they targeted businesses that were part of national chains. Fearing boycotts in the North, these chains began to desegregate their businesses.

Freedom Riders were treated very harshly by Southern law enforcement officers. Again, many of these law enforcement officers were members of the Ku Klux Klan. In Birmingham, Alabama, the Public Safety commissioner gave KKK members fifteen minutes to attack an incoming group of Freedom Riders before having police protect them. These riders were severely beaten and one man (a white civil rights activist) required fifty stitches in his head. All over the South, hundreds of Freedom Riders were jailed and were then treated very harshly in jail. They were crammed into tiny, filthy cells, and sporadically beaten.

On May 29, 1961, Attorney General Robert Kennedy sent a petition to the Interstate Commerce Commission (ICC) asking it to comply with the bus desegregation ruling it had issued in November 1955.

In September, CORE and SNCC leaders began planning a mass demonstration because the ICC had not responded to Robert Kennedy's petition. The planners' intention was to mobilize hundreds, possibly thousands, of nonviolent demonstrators to converge on Washington, DC, to apply pressure on the ICC and the Kennedy administration. Planning stopped at the end of September when the ICC issued orders to have the position it had taken in 1955 enforced. The new policy went into effect on November 1, 1961. Once the ICC rule began to be enforced, passengers sat wherever they wanted on interstate buses and trains; "white" and "colored" signs were removed from terminals; and drinking fountains, restrooms, waiting areas, and lunch counters in bus terminals were no longer segregated.

The Freedom Rides, and the violent reactions they provoked, bolstered the credibility of the Civil Rights Movement. They called national attention to the way law enforcement officers in the South disregarded federal laws and used violence to enforce local Jim Crow laws. In addition, the fact that Freedom Riders were northerners who faced danger on behalf of southern blacks impressed many blacks throughout the South and inspired them to engage in direct action for civil rights. They then formed the backbone of the wider civil rights movement. This eventually led to the passage of the Civil Rights Act of 1964.

## Still Not Enough

Though the Civil Rights Act of 1964 was most definitely landmark legislation, it did not remove the obstacles black men encountered at the polls when trying to vote. Though they had been given the right to vote by the federal government with the passage of the Fifteenth Amendment to the Constitution in 1870, individual states and localities still had the authority to establish and administer their own voting requirements. The Civil Rights Act of 1964 did not change this. Still more legislation was needed, which meant still more protest was needed.

Civil rights workers stepped up to the plate with their uncommon courage and undying perseverance and were able to influence legislators to pass the Voting Rights Act of 1965. This law removed the legal barriers at state and local levels which had been preventing black men from exercising their right to vote. The Voting Rights Act prohibited state and local governments from imposing any voting law that resulted in discrimination against racial or language minorities. It also contained a provision prohibiting certain jurisdictions from implementing any change affecting voting without receiving preapproval from the US Attorney General or the US District Court for District of Columbia.

The Voting Rights Act of 1965 gave black voters the legal means to challenge voting restrictions and vastly improved voter turnout. It also specifically allowed black women to vote.

## Intervening Years

When black women were excluded from the benefits of the Nineteenth Amendment to the Constitution in 1920, they, like white suffragists before them, did not passively sit back and wait to see if they were going to be allowed to vote. They continued their campaign to be seen as equal to both men and other women as evidenced by obtaining the right to vote. Black women in all parts of the United States found themselves confronting a number of methods aimed at stopping them from voting. These methods included having to wait in line for up to twelve hours to register to vote, pay head taxes, and undergo new tests. One of the new tests required that they read and interpret the Constitution before being deemed eligible to vote. In the South, black women faced even more severe obstacles to voting. These obstacles included bodily harm and fabricated charges designed to land them in jail if they attempted to vote. This treatment of black women continued in the South until 1965 when President Lyndon Johnson signed the Voting Rights Act into law.

## Phase Two

Once the right to vote was obtained for *all* women, the women's movement began its second phase (1960s to 1990s), focusing on other issues contributing to women's inequality with men. This phase of the women's movement resulted in:

marital rape laws; establishment of rape crisis centers and battered women's shelters; changes in custody and divorce laws; equal pay for equal work standards; equal credit opportunities; establishment of a law requiring US military academies to accept women; integration of not only the military academies, but also the armed forces, NASA, single sex colleges, men's clubs and the Supreme Court.

Due to the success of the second phase of the women's movement, the number of women in government and traditionally male-dominated fields dramatically increased, and the salary of the average American woman also increased. However, in 2008 the average woman's salary was still only 77 percent of the average man's salary for the same job. In 2015, women were *still* not earning the same pay as men for the same work across the board. President Obama addressed this in his 2015 State of the Union Address, advocating for equal pay for equal work legislation.

*Personal note:* I think it is absolutely criminal and/or sinful that equal pay for equal work has to be legislated. This is an example of an "ism" heart condition.

## The True Emancipator

Though Abraham Lincoln is known as the Great Emancipator, there is one who came before him who is the true emancipator. His name is Jesus Christ. When Jesus walked the earth in the flesh, he "traveled throughout the region of Galilee, teaching in the synagogues and announcing the Good News about the Kingdom. And he healed every kind of disease and illness" (Matthew 4:23).

Early in his ministry, Jesus told his family, friends, and neighbors very clearly who he was and what he was about to do.

> When he came to the village of Nazareth, his boyhood home, he went as usual to the synagogue on the Sabbath and stood up to read the Scriptures. The scroll of Isaiah the prophet was handed to him. He unrolled the scroll and found the place where this was written: "The Spirit of the LORD is upon me, for he has anointed me to bring Good News to the poor. He has sent me to proclaim that captives will be released, that the blind will see, that the oppressed will be set free, and that the time of the LORD's favor has come." He rolled up the scroll, handed it back to the attendant, and sat down. All eyes in the synagogue looked at him intently. Then he began to speak to them. "The Scripture you've just heard has been fulfilled this very day!" (Luke 4:16–21)

Soon after this, he told a group of Pharisees (Jewish religious leaders), "The thief comes only to steal and kill and destroy; I came that they may have life, and have it abundantly" (John 10:10 RSV).

When you look at the diseases and illnesses Jesus healed, it becomes clear that he was setting people free from all kinds of physical bondage (paralysis, demonic possession, leprosy, blindness, even death) so they could live a life of abundance. When you look at how he related to women and treated women throughout his earthly ministry, it also becomes clear that he set women free from the oppression of cultural expectations so they too could live abundant lives.

> Soon afterward Jesus began a tour of the nearby towns and villages, preaching and announcing the Good News about the Kingdom of God. He took his twelve disciples with him, along with some women who had been cured of evil spirits and diseases. Among them were Mary Magdalene, from whom he had cast out seven demons; Joanna, the wife of Chuza, Herod's business manager; Susanna; and many others who were contributing from their own resources to support Jesus and his disciples. (Luke 8:1–3)

Since Jesus apparently included women in his inner circle, we can surmise he did not demand women fit into the limited, rigid roles their culture expected of them. Rather, he set them free from the bondage of cultural expectations and allowed and/or encouraged them to be who they had been created to be.

I find it incredibly sad that the church, his hands, feet and heart in the world, did not follow his example in setting woman free from the bondage of cultural expectations.

# CHAPTER FOUR

# HOW GOD SEES WOMEN

The culture in biblical times was a rigidly patriarchal one in which men treated women as property. Women were identified by the men in whose household they lived (the daughter of so-and-so, the wife of so-and-so). They were bought, sold, traded, and given away, just like other property the men owned. Women had no say over their own destinies. They were seen by men to have no inherent value.

God, however, saw women as valuable. Throughout the Old Testament he picked women on numerous occasions to execute important and strategic actions in his plan for his people. A few of these women were Rahab, Deborah, Huldah, and Esther.

## Background

As recorded in the book of Genesis, God sent a flood to cover the earth and destroy all living things because the people had done evil in his sight. The only ones who survived the flood were Noah and his family. Noah's descendants eventually scattered all over the known world. Sometime later, God chose one of these families to be his chosen people, his family, and he chose Abram to be the father of his family. He told Abram "Leave your native country, your relatives, and your father's family, and go to the land that I will show you. I will make you into a great nation. I will bless you and make you famous, and you will be a blessing to others" (Genesis 12:1–2). Abram obeyed and he eventually reached the land of Canaan. When he got there, God said to him, "Look as far as you can see in every direction–north and south, east and west. I am giving all this land, as far as you can see, to you and your descendants as a permanent possession" (Genesis 13:14–15). "Then the LORD said to Abram, 'You can be sure that your descendants will be strangers in a foreign land, where they will be oppressed as slaves for four hundred years. . . . After four generations your descendants will return here to this land'" (Genesis 15:13, 16).

The foreign land the people of Israel inhabited as slaves was Egypt. When the Lord deemed it was time for his people to return to Canaan, the land he had promised Abram would forever belong to his descendants, he appointed Moses to lead the people out of Egypt. Moses did indeed lead the people of Israel out of Egypt. He, however, did not lead them into the Promised Land. Joshua did that.

## Rahab Enters the Picture

Then Joshua secretly sent out two spies from the Israelite camp at Acacia Grove. He instructed them, "Scout out the land on the other side of the Jordan River, especially around Jericho." So the two men set out and came to the house of a prostitute named Rahab and stayed there that night.

But someone told the king of Jericho, "Some Israelites have come here tonight to spy out the land." So the king of Jericho sent orders to Rahab: "Bring out the men who have come into your house, for they have come to spy out the whole land."

Rahab had hidden the two men, but she replied, "Yes, the men were here earlier, but I didn't know where they were from. They left the town at dusk, as the gates were about to close. I don't know where they went." . . . Then, since Rahab's house was built into the town wall, she let them down by a rope through the window. . . . Then the two spies came down from the hill country, crossed the Jordan River, and reported to Joshua all that had happened to them. (Joshua 2:1–5, 15, 23)

The Jordan River bordered the Promised Land. When the Israelites crossed the Jordan River and entered the Promised Land, they were faced with many walled cities full of enemies. The first city was Jericho. This was a critical time in the journey of God's people from slavery to freedom, and who did God call on to help his people at this critical time? He called on a woman, a prostitute!

The battle for Jericho ensued and resulted in the Israelites taking possession of the city. When the battle ended,

The men who had been spies went in and brought out Rahab, her father, mother, brothers, and all the other relatives who were with her. They moved her whole family to a safe place near the camp of Israel. . . .

So Joshua spared Rahab the prostitute and her relatives who were with her in the house, because she had hidden the spies Joshua sent to Jericho. (Joshua 6:23, 25)

Approximately one century after Rahab lived, God chose to use another woman, Deborah, in a very powerful way. Her story is told in the fourth and fifth chapters of the book of Judges.

## Background

Following the Israelite conquest of the land of Canaan, God's people settled into their lives in the land he had promised them long before. They did not, however, consistently follow his commandments and live the life he had called them to live. They fell into a four-part cyclical pattern of (1) moving away from God and worshipping idols; (2) being conquered and enslaved by an enemy nation; (3) crying out to God for help and deliverance; and (4) God answering their call by sending a leader to bring them back to him. The people would then return to him for a while. This never lasted though. They would eventually move away from him and start the cycle all over again. This cycle repeated itself over and over again. God tried for a very long time to get his people back on track by sending many leaders, or judges, and prophets to help them and to warn them. Though some of these godly leaders were able to lead the Israelites back to God, the people never stayed there for very long. They continually drifted back into doing whatever they wanted, ignoring God's rules and expectations.

## Enter Deborah

After Ehud's death, the Israelites again did evil in the LORD's sight. So the LORD turned them over to King Jabin of Hazor, a Canaanite king. The commander of his army was Sisera. . . . Sisera, who had 900 iron chariots, ruthlessly oppressed the Israelites for twenty years. Then the people of Israel cried out to the LORD for help.

Deborah, the wife of Lappidoth, was a prophet who was judging Israel at that time. She would sit under the Palm of Deborah, between Ramah and Bethel in the hill country of Ephraim, and the Israelites would go to her for judgment. One day she sent for Barak. . . . She said to him, "This is what the LORD, the God of Israel, commands you: Call out 10,000 warriors from the tribes of Naphtali and Zebulum at Mount Tabor. And I will call out Sisera, commander of Jabin's army, along with his chariots and warriors, to the Kishon River. There I will give you victory over him."

Barak told her, "I will go, but only if you go with me." (Judges 4: 1–8)

The Israelite army did engage the army of Sisera in battle. Before the Israelites marched into battle though, Deborah said to Barak, "Get ready! This is the day the LORD will give you victory over Sisera, for the LORD is marching ahead of you" (Judges 4:14). The Israelite army did indeed prevail over the army of Sisera, just as Deborah had prophesied.

Deborah is certainly a unique figure in the history of Israel. When she is first introduced in Scripture, she is identified as a wife and then as a prophet. Introducing her as the wife of Lappidoth is consistent with the culture of the time. Introducing her as a prophet establishes her leadership as based on a personal relationship with God in which he chose her to speak for him, conveying messages to his people. The people of Israel must have recognized that she was chosen by God to speak for him, or she would not have had the obvious authority she had, as well as the respect of the people.

Approximately seven hundred years after Deborah lived, God chose yet another woman, Huldah, to be a prophet.

## Background

By this time the nation of Israel had been split into two kingdoms: the northern kingdom (Israel) and the southern kingdom (Judah). The people of both kingdoms continually engaged in the four-part cyclical pattern of disobeying God's commands, coming under the control of another nation, repenting, and God sending someone to lead them back to him. God finally had enough of this repetitive pattern and decided that his people—his children—needed serious discipline. He chose destruction and exile as his methods of disciplining his children. He exiled Israel to Assyria about 722–721 BC and he exiled Judah to Babylon about 587–586 BC. Huldah lived in Judah during the period of time after Israel had been exiled to Assyria and before Judah was exiled to Babylon. King Josiah was ruler of Judah during Huldah's lifetime. Huldah's story is told in 2 Kings 22 and 2 Chronicles 34.

## Enter Huldah

During King Josiah's reign, a priest "found the Book of the Law of the LORD that was written by Moses" (2 Chronicles 34:14). It was found while repairs were being done on the temple and is believed to be what later became the book of Deuteronomy, the fifth book of the Old Testament. The book, which was in the form of a scroll at the time, was taken to the king and read to him. "When the king heard what was written in the Law, he tore his clothes in despair" (2 Chronicles 34:19). He had not realized until then just how far off track, how out-of-sync with God's commands, his people really were. He then sent some of his most trusted advisors "to consult with the prophet Huldah. She was the wife of Shallum" (2 Chronicles 34:22).

> She said to them, "The LORD, the God of Israel, has spoken! Go back and tell the man who sent you, 'This is what the LORD says: I am going to bring disaster on this city and its people. All the curses written in the scroll that was read to the king of Judah will come true. For

my people have abandoned me and offered sacrifices to pagan gods, and I am very angry with them for everything they have done. My anger will be poured out on this place, and it will not be quenched.'

"But go to the king of Judah who sent you to seek the LORD and tell him: 'This is what the LORD, the God of Israel, says concerning the message you have just heard: You were sorry and humbled yourself before God when you heard his words against this city and its people. You humbled yourself and tore your clothing in despair and wept before me in repentance. And I have indeed heard you, says the LORD. So I will not send the promised disaster until after you have died and been buried in peace. You yourself will not see the disaster I am going to bring on this city and its people.'" (2 Chronicles 34:23–28)

When Josiah heard this, he instituted major religious reforms throughout his kingdom. "So Josiah removed all detestable idols from the entire land of Israel and required everyone to worship the LORD their God. And throughout the rest of his lifetime, they did not turn away from the LORD, the God of their ancestors" (2 Chronicles 34:33).

Josiah was killed during a battle with the Assyrian army. The next two kings led the people away from God once again. The second king's reign was followed by the Babylonian exile.

In keeping with the culture of the time, Huldah, like Deborah before her, was identified as both a prophet and a wife when first introduced in Scripture. This would seem to indicate that she successfully lived out both her role as prophet and her role as wife. In their book *Women of the Bible* Sue Poorman Richards and Lawrence Richards note, "A woman can have a ministry and still win a reputation as a good wife. Marriage and ministry are not necessarily in conflict."[21]

When considering what exceptional women Deborah and Huldah were in light of the culture in which they lived, it is important not to overlook what exceptional men Barak and Josiah were. Both men were unique figures in the history of Israel due to their willingness to submit to the leadership of a woman.

Barak's insistence that Deborah accompany him into battle seemingly conveys his deep respect for her and his trust in her relationship with God.

Josiah intentionally seeking spiritual counsel from a female prophet during a time when four male prophets (Jeremiah, Zephaniah, Nahum, and Habbakuk) were living is nothing short of amazing. What is even more amazing is that King Josiah not only sought the counsel of a woman, he acted on it, instituting very radical reforms. Josiah must have seen something in Huldah similar to what Barak saw in Deborah. Scot McKnight, in *The Blue Parakeet*, states, "Huldah is not chosen because no men were available; she is chosen because she is truly exceptional among the prophets."[22]

Esther lived approximately 150 years after Huldah. As he had done with Rahab, Deborah, and Huldah, God once again chose a woman to play a critical role in the story of his people, delivering them from destruction once again.

## Background

God eventually brought to an end the disciplining process of the peoples of Israel and of Judah and facilitated their return to their homeland. Many Jews, however, did not return to their homeland. Esther grew up in Babylon in the Jewish community who chose not to return to their homeland when the time of exile was over. Babylon was, at that time, under the control of Persia and was ruled by King Xerxes.

## Enter Esther

> At that time there was a Jewish man in the fortress of Susa whose name was Mordecai. . . . His family had been among those who . . . had been exiled from Jerusalem to Babylon . . . . This man had a very beautiful and lovely young cousin, Hadassah, who was also called Esther. When her father and mother died, Mordecai adopted her into his family and raised her as his own daughter. (Esther 2:5–7)

In the meantime, Queen Vashti incurred the wrath of her husband, King Xerxes, and was deposed as queen. Many young women were then brought to the fortress of Susa so the king could choose a new queen from among them. Esther was one of these young women. "Esther had not told anyone of her nationality and family background, because Mordecai had directed her not to do so" (Esther 2:10). "Esther was taken to King Xerxes at the royal palace in early winter of the seventh year of his reign. And the king loved Esther more than any of the other young women. He was so delighted with her that he set the royal crown on her head and declared her queen instead of Vashti" (Esther 2:16–17).

Sometime after Esther became queen, Mordecai became a palace official. It was known that he was a Jew. However, no one at the palace knew of the familial relationship between Mordecai and Esther. Mordecai then incurred the wrath of the king's second in command, Haman. "He had learned of Mordecai's nationality, so he decided it was not enough to lay hands on Mordecai alone. Instead, he looked for a way to destroy all the Jews throughout the entire empire of Xerxes" (Esther 3:6). One year later, Haman influenced Xerxes to issue a decree. "Dispatches were sent by swift messengers into all the provinces of the empire, giving the order that all Jews—young and old, including women and children—must be killed, slaughtered, and annihilated on a single day. . . . At the king's command, the decree went out by swift messengers, and it was also proclaimed in the fortress of Susa. Then the king and Haman sat down to drink, but the city of Susa fell into confusion" (Esther 3:13, 15).

When Mordecai learned of this, he asked Esther to go to the king and intercede for her people. Esther replied, "All the king's officials and even the people in the provinces know that anyone who appears before the king in his inner court without being invited is doomed to die unless the king holds out his gold scepter. And the king has not called for me to come to him for thirty days" (Esther 4:11).

Mordecai and Esther dialogued back and forth about it for a while. At one point, Mordecai said to Esther, "Who knows if perhaps you were made queen for just such a time as this?" (Esther 4:14).

Esther did eventually go to the king and intercede for her people. In response, King Xerxes had Haman executed and issued a second decree giving Jews in all his provinces permission to unite and defend their lives. This is exactly what they did and they were successful in overpowering their enemies.

The stories of how God used these four women certainly seems to indicate that, though the Old Testament Hebrew culture was a rigidly patriarchal one in which women were viewed as property with no inherent value, God views women as valuable and competent.

# CHAPTER FIVE

# SOLOMON'S WORDS

Solomon lived after Deborah and before Huldah. He was a man of great wisdom. As stated above, Deborah was one of many prophets God sent to his people to lead them back to him. The people of Israel eventually grew tired of this style of leadership and asked to have a king so they could be like the nations around them. This occurred toward the end of the life of Samuel the prophet.

> As Samuel grew old, he appointed his sons to be judges over Israel. Joel and Abijah, his oldest sons, held court in Beersheba. But they were not like their father, for they were greedy for money. They accepted bribes and perverted justice.
>
> Finally, all the elders of Israel met at Ramah to discuss the matter with Samuel. "Look," they told him, "you are now old, and your sons are not like you. Give us a king to judge us like all the other nations have."

Samuel was displeased with their request and went to the LORD for guidance. "Do everything they say to you," the LORD replied, "for they are rejecting me, not you. They don't want me to be their king any longer. Ever since I brought them from Egypt they have continually abandoned me and followed other gods. And now they are giving you the same treatment. Do as they ask." (1 Samuel 8:1–9)

The first king of Israel was Saul. David was the second. Solomon, David's son, was the third.

Fairly early in his reign as king "the LORD appeared to Solomon in a dream, and God said, 'What do you want? Ask, and I will give it to you!'" (1 Kings 3:5). Solomon's response was "Give me an understanding heart so that I can govern your people well and know the difference between right and wrong. For who by himself is able to govern this great people of yours?" (1 Kings 3:9). God was delighted that Solomon had asked for wisdom rather than riches and fame. As a matter of fact, God was so delighted that he gave Solomon what he asked for (wisdom) and what he had not asked for (riches and fame).

## A Guidebook

Solomon is credited with having written most of the book of Proverbs. It is a book of wisdom, written as a guidebook to help people navigate their day-to-day lives in skillful, healthy ways.

Chapter 31 of the book of Proverbs describes a woman who has often been held up to Christian women everywhere by church leaders as a model to which they are expected to aspire. Chapter 31 begins with the words "The Sayings of King Lemuel." There is no definitive historical account regarding the identity of King Lemuel. Because King Lemuel is not listed among the kings of Judah or Israel, some biblical scholars believe that Lemuel was actually a pen name for Solomon and that chapter 31, like most of the book of Proverbs, was actually written by Solomon.

This is the Proverbs 31 picture of an ideal woman:

Who can find a virtuous and capable wife?
　　She is more precious than rubies.
Her husband can trust her,
　　and she will greatly enrich his life.
She brings him good, not harm,
　　all the days of her life.

She finds wool and flax
　　and busily spins it.
She is like a merchant's ship,
　　bringing her food from afar.
She gets up before dawn to prepare breakfast
　　for her household
　　and plan the day's work for her servant girls.

She goes to inspect a field and buys it;
　　with her earnings she plants a vineyard.
She is energetic and strong,
　　a hard worker.

She makes sure her dealings are profitable;
  her lamp burns late into the night.


Her hands are busy spinning thread,
  her fingers twisting fiber.
She extends a helping hand to the poor
  and opens her arms to the needy.
She has no fear of winter for her household,
  for everyone has warm clothes.

She makes her own bedspreads.
She dresses in fine linen and purple gowns. . . .
She makes belted linen garments
  and sashes to sell to the merchants.

She is clothed with strength and dignity,
  and she laughs without fear of the future.
When she speaks, her words are wise,
  and she gives instructions with kindness.
She carefully watches everything in her
    household
  and suffers nothing from laziness.
  (Proverbs 31:10–22, 24–27)

When this Scripture passage is unpacked verse by verse, it is obvious that the woman described in Proverbs 31 is:

- skilled and competent (verse 10: She is a "capable wife.")

- trustworthy (verse 11: "Her husband can trust her.")

- resourceful and hardworking (verses 13–14: "She finds wool and flax and busily spins it. She is like a merchant's ship, bringing her food from afar.")

- energetic, organized, a planner and has others working for her (verse 15: "She gets up before dawn to . . . plan the day's work for her servant girls.")

- an entrepreneur and a decision maker (verse 16: "She goes to inspect a field and buys it; with her earnings she plants a vineyard.")

- a shrewd and successful businessperson (verse 18: "She makes sure her dealings are profitable.")

- diligent (verse 18: "Her lamp burns late into the night.")

- generous (verse 20: "She extends a helping hand to the poor and opens her arms to the needy.")

- takes good care of her family (verse 15: "She gets up . . . to prepare breakfast for her household"; and verse 21: "She has no fear of winter for her household, for everyone has warm clothes.")

- industrious (verse 22: "She makes her own bedspreads.")

- a fashionable dresser (verse 22: "She dresses in fine linen and purple gowns.")

- strong, dignified, and confident (verse 25: "She is clothed with strength and dignity, and she laughs without fear of the future.")

- thoughtful, wise, kind (verse 26: "When she speaks, her words are wise, and she gives instructions with kindness.")

- thorough (verse 27: "She carefully watches everything in her household and suffers nothing from laziness.")

Since Solomon's wisdom was God-given, it is not much of a stretch to regard Solomon as a channel through which God communicated his own wisdom to the world. It is not much more of a stretch then, to consider the qualities listed above to be the qualities God admires and values in women. Take note, I said women, plural, not woman, singular.

J. Lee Grady, in his book *10 Lies the Church Tells Women*, states:

> We need to understand that the Proverbs 31 woman was never meant to be interpreted as

normative for every Christian woman. The Hebrew poetry employed in this passage of Proverbs is an acrostic; each verse begins with a different letter of the Hebrew alphabet and describes some aspect of a godly woman's life. The woman described here is actually a composite—the passage was never meant to describe one woman. (If it were, she would indeed be an Old Testament superwoman, since she never seems to sleep or stop working!) Christian women who uphold the Proverbs 31 woman as a virtuous ideal must realize that God does not expect them to emulate her unrealistic schedule—because she is actually several "model" women rolled into one.[23]

Grady goes on to say:

Traditionalists who champion this verse as a picture of the happy housewife would probably not endorse the lifestyle of this woman if they met her on the street. In her ancient Middle Eastern society, she was an entrepreneur. She stayed occupied with her home-based business day and night—and someone else probably watched her children when she was selling linen in the marketplace, dealing with merchants, buying fields, or making wine with the fruit of her vineyard. She was most definitely not a stay-at-home mom.[24]

I believe God wants us to emulate these qualities, to the best of our abilities in whatever specific way he has called us to live, remembering that we don't have to do this alone. We have the help, guidance, and most of all, the power of the Holy Spirit to help us at every step along the way.

God has not set an impossibly high standard for his daughters to live by so he can torture us and punish us when we fail to meet the standard. Rather, he set this standard for us to live by so the world will know that we are his daughters. He wants us to live by a different standard—a higher standard—than the world lives by so we can be identified by those around us as belonging to God and living our lives for him. It is not our responsibility or our duty to fit into the mold our society or our culture says we must fit into. It is our responsibility and our duty to follow the leading of the Holy Spirit and to adjust our life according to his directives. In his book *The Blue Parakeet* Scot McKnight says, "Adaptability and development are woven into the very fabric of the Bible. From beginning to end there is a pattern of adopting and adapting. It is the attempt to foist one person's days and ways on everyone's days and ways that quenches the Holy Spirit."[25]

# CHAPTER SIX

# THE PATTERN CONTINUED

When Jesus came to earth in a physical body, he saw women as valuable and treated them as such. He did not see women as property and did not treat them as property.

Mary of Bethany was one woman whose value Jesus affirmed, and whom he set free to follow her heart rather than abide by cultural expectations. Mary of Bethany was the sister of Martha and Lazarus. Jesus seems to have had a special relationship with these three siblings during his earthly ministry. John 11:1–45 recounts the story of Jesus raising Lazarus from the dead. Note the following phrases from that account:

- "The two sisters sent a message to Jesus telling him, 'Lord, your dear friend is very sick.'" (verse 3)

- "Although Jesus loved Martha, Mary, and Lazarus . . ." (verse 5)

- "'Where have you put him?' he asked them.
They told him, 'Lord, come and see.' Then
Jesus wept. The people who were standing
nearby said, 'See how much he loved him!'"
(verses 34–36)

Seeing how Jesus responds to Mary of Bethany in the
following account, we get a glimpse into how Jesus viewed
and treated women as a whole.

As Jesus and the disciples continued on their
way to Jerusalem, they came to a certain village
where a woman named Martha welcomed
him into her home. Her sister, Mary, sat at
the Lord's feet, listening to what he taught.
But Martha was distracted by the big dinner
she was preparing. She came to Jesus and said,
"Lord, doesn't it seem unfair to you that my
sister just sits here while I do all the work? Tell
her to come and help me."
But the Lord said to her, "My dear
Martha, you are worried and upset over all
these details! There is only one thing worth
being concerned about. Mary has discovered
it, and it will not be taken away from her."
(Luke 10:38–42)

If we don't keep in mind the differences between the
Jewish culture of Jesus's day and our modern culture, we
miss the impact of this Scripture passage. The response Jesus
gave to Martha was totally unexpected. It flew in the face of

accepted cultural roles and norms. Jesus made it absolutely clear that women not only belong in the kitchen, they also belong in his classroom. Sarah Sumner, in her book *Men and Women in the Church*, makes this point when she says, "We may assume that it was no big deal for Jesus to teach Mary about eternal things because it's normal for women to be educated today. But indeed, it was extraordinary. Other rabbis shunned the idea of teaching a woman. Jesus was the first rabbi ever to accept a woman student."[26]

This was not the last extraordinary event that took place that day. Mary actually had the audacity to not only let herself be taught by Jesus rather than help prepare the meal, she was even assertive enough to anoint Jesus during the meal.

> A dinner was prepared in Jesus' honor. Martha served, and Lazarus was among those who ate with him. Then Mary took a twelve-ounce jar of expensive perfume made from essence of nard, and she anointed Jesus' feet with it, wiping his feet with her hair. The house was filled with the fragrance.
>
> But Judas Iscariot, the disciple who would soon betray him, said, "That perfume was worth a year's wages. It should have been sold and the money given to the poor." . . . Jesus replied, "Leave her alone. She did this in preparation for my burial. You will always have the poor among you, but you will not always have me." (John 12:2–5, 7–8)

Again Jesus came to Mary's defense. By doing that, he clearly gave her permission to follow her heart rather than following societal expectations.

## Another Mary

Mary Magdalene was another woman who was a disciple of Jesus. She is mentioned in all four gospels. Jesus freed her from the grip of demonic possession. She then followed him faithfully. Luke 8:1–3 tells us, "Jesus began a tour of the nearby towns and villages, preaching and announcing the Good News about the Kingdom of God. He took his twelve disciples with him, along with some women who had been cured of evil spirits and diseases. Among them were Mary Magdalene, from whom he had cast out seven demons." Mary followed Jesus devotedly from the time she was set free up to and including his crucifixion. "Standing near the cross were Jesus' mother, and his mother's sister, Mary (the wife of Clopas), and Mary Magdalene" (John 19:25).

As we know, Jesus died on Friday afternoon. Once it was confirmed that he was indeed dead, Joseph of Arimathea took his body down from the cross and prepared his body for burial according to Jewish culture. He then placed Jesus's body in a tomb.

> Early on Sunday morning, while it was still dark, Mary Magdalene came to the tomb and found that the stone had been rolled away from the entrance. She ran and found Simon Peter and the other disciple, the one whom Jesus loved. She said, "They have taken the

Lord's body out of the tomb, and we don't know where they have put him!"

Peter and the other disciple started out for the tomb. They were both running, but the other disciple outran Peter and reached the tomb first. He stooped and looked in and saw the linen wrappings lying there, but he didn't go in. Then Simon Peter arrived and went inside. He also noticed the linen wrappings lying there, while the cloth that had covered Jesus' head was folded up and lying apart from the other wrappings. Then the disciple who had reached the tomb first also went in, and he saw and believed—for until then they still hadn't understood the Scriptures that said Jesus must rise from the dead. Then they went home.

Mary was standing outside the tomb crying, and as she wept, she stooped and looked in. She saw two white-robed angels, one sitting at the head and the other at the foot of the place where the body of Jesus had been lying. "Dear woman, why are you crying?" the angels asked her.

"Because they have taken away my Lord," she replied, "and I don't know where they have put him."

She turned to leave and saw someone standing there. It was Jesus, but she didn't recognize him. "Dear woman, why are you crying?" Jesus asked her. "Who are you looking for?"

She thought he was the gardener. "Sir, she said, "if you have taken him away, tell me where you have put him, and I will go and get him."

"Mary!" Jesus said.

She turned to him and cried out, "Rabboni!" (which is Hebrew for "Teacher"). (John 20:1–16)

Again, if we don't keep in mind the differences between the Jewish culture of Jesus's day and our modern culture, we miss the significance of the choice Jesus made regarding to whom he first appeared after his resurrection. He could have appeared to Peter or to John (the disciple whom Jesus loved). Either of these choices would have made sense as they were both part of the twelve and were both destined to be key players in the establishment of Jesus's church on earth. Jesus, however, chose not to appear to one or both of these men first. He chose instead to appear to one of his women disciples. Inherent in this choice, I believe, is a powerful nonverbal statement about the value Jesus placed on his women disciples. He clearly saw them as equal partners in ministry with his male disciples.

A fact of Scripture which lends further weight to this claim, I believe, is that Mary Magdalene was not only the first person to whom the risen Jesus appeared, she was also the first individual that Jesus commissioned to spread the gospel—the good news that death had not defeated him, that he was alive! "'Don't cling to me,' Jesus said, 'for I haven't yet ascended to the Father. But go find my brothers and tell them, "I am ascending to my Father and your Father, to my God and your God."' Mary Magdalene found the disciples and told them, 'I have seen the Lord!' Then she gave them his message" (John 20:17–18).

## The Pattern Continued

The pattern that Jesus set regarding how he saw and how he treated women in his ministry, setting them free from the bondage of cultural expectations, continued after his death and resurrection. The book of Acts tells us "They all met together and were constantly united in prayer, along with Mary the mother of Jesus, several other women, and the brothers of Jesus. During this time, when about 120 believers were together in one place, Peter stood up and addressed them" (Acts 1:14–15). This Scripture passage is discussed in the book *Women of the Bible*.

> What is significant here is the simple phrase "the women." When the Jews gathered for study or prayer, it was a meeting of men. It took ten men, a *minyan*, to convene for worship in Judaism, and in this case women literally did not "count." Yet here we see the followers of Christ assembled to pray and not only are women among them, but verse 15 counts them among the 120 "disciples" who were present. While modern readers would likely pass over these two words, they reflect

a radical change in first-century attitude. Believers had gathered for prayer and worship, and the text specifically says that "the women" were among them. . . . The first mention in Acts of women pictures them gathered with men, for prayer and worship. This scene alone indicates that the new freedom Christ offered to women had begun to be experienced by those who trusted in Him.[27]

The apostle Paul, following the example Jesus and his disciples set, also saw women as equal partners and coworkers in ministry, and treated them as such. "Paul envisioned a world in which Jews and Greeks, educated and barbarian, slaves and free, men and women would be equal citizens in a kingdom that was not political but spiritual."[28] In his letters to some of the churches he planted, Paul mentions numerous women who served in key leadership positions in the new congregations. The only woman who will be discussed here however, is Priscilla. Paul mentions her in his letter to the church in Rome. "Give my greetings to Priscilla and Aquila, my co-workers in the ministry of Christ Jesus" (Romans 16:3).

Sue Poorman Richards and Lawrence Richards, in *Women of the Bible*, share this:

> Priscilla and her husband [Aquila] were Christian Jews who met Paul in Corinth. . . . When Paul left Corinth after a ministry of some two to three years, Priscilla and Aquila

went with him to Ephesus. There they hosted a house-church in their home, as they probably did in both Rome and Corinth.

. . . As a Jewish wife, Priscilla would have been expected to be subject to her husband. Aquila would have been the one who studied God's Law and who sat with the other men in the synagogue. Priscilla would have been expected to know the laws governing a kosher kitchen, but in all other matters she would have been expected to defer to her husband. In mentioning the couple, if both were mentioned at all, normal mode of speech would have identified Aquila "and his wife."

But here in the New Testament not only is Priscilla identified by name, she is frequently mentioned first.

. . . The easy exchange of the names of Priscilla and Aquila makes it clear that Priscilla was a full partner with her husband in ministry. . . .

Aquila and Priscilla's marriage exemplifies the elevated social status restored to women by the gospel of Christ. The new faith exalted women, making them partners in ministry as well as in life.[29]

In his book *10 Lies the Church Tells Women* J. Lee Grady states, "Nowhere in the Bible are women called to be weak. A careful study of women in Scripture reveals that the godly women who served His purpose in their generation displayed courage, endured hardship, and exercised the kind of faith that overcomes impossible odds."[30] I highlighted a few of these women; however, if you peruse the Bible, you will find women of faith, courage, and daring throughout it from beginning to end. They are as varied in personality styles, spiritual gifts, and callings as today's Christian women.

It is unfortunate, to put it very mildly, that church leaders have historically refused to view women through God's eyes, and because of this have not followed the example set by Jesus, Paul, and other early church leaders in allowing and encouraging women to serve in all levels and roles in ministry.

# CHAPTER SEVEN

# HOW THE CHURCH FAILED WOMEN

The church failed women by not taking the lead in setting them free. Rather than setting an example for the world to follow, as Jesus and Paul did, the church has chosen to view and treat women as the world has.

## One More Mary

I, like Mary of Bethany and Mary Magdalene, am a Christ follower. As such, I value the words Jesus spoke during his earthly ministry. The particular words I value above all others, the words I use as a plumb line for my life, are those which comprise his most famous sermon, the Sermon on the Mount, found in Matthew 5:1—7:29. (See appendix one.)

There are two things that stand out for me about this sermon. The first is that he does not mention anything about race, gender, or social class. The second is that he tells us, his followers, to be a light in the world.

You are the light of the world—like a city on a hilltop that cannot be hidden. No one lights a lamp and then puts it under a basket. Instead, a lamp is placed on a stand, where it gives light to everyone in the house. In the same way, let your good deeds shine out for all to see, so that everyone will praise your heavenly Father. (Matthew 5:14–16)

## Light

The image of light shows up at several significant places in the Bible. When the Israelites left Egypt under Moses's leadership, "The LORD went ahead of them. He guided them during the day with a pillar of cloud, and he provided light at night with a pillar of fire. This allowed them to travel by day or by night. And the LORD did not remove the pillar of cloud or pillar of fire from its place in front of the people" (Exodus 13:21–22).

When Jesus came to earth in a physical body, he said that *he* was the light. "Jesus spoke to the people once more and said, 'I am the light of the world. If you follow me, you won't have to walk in darkness, because you will have the light that leads to life'" (John 8:12). When speaking to a crowd in Jerusalem after his triumphal entry into the city, five days before his death, he said,

"My light will shine for you just a little longer. Walk in the light while you can, so the darkness will not overtake you. Those who walk in the darkness cannot see where they are going. Put

your trust in the light while there is still time;
then you will become children of the light."
(John 12:35–36)

"If you trust me, you are trusting not only me,
but also God who sent me. For when you see
me, you are seeing the one who sent me. I have
come as a light to shine in this dark world,
so that all who put their trust in me will no
longer remain in the dark." (John 12:44–46)

When Jesus's earthly body died he could no longer
carry the light, therefore he planted light inside his followers
and clearly instructed us to let that light, *his* light, shine.

Jesus wants his followers (individual, congregational,
and denominational) to be bright shining lights in the
world. He wants his church to be a light which shines so
bright it stands out in the world as different and wonderful.
As a matter of fact, his church is supposed to be so different
and so wonderful that it will draw people to it who will ask
what makes it so different.

## Not of This World

As you read the Sermon on the Mount and ponder the
lifestyle Jesus modeled and calls us to live, it becomes clear
that God's standards in no way, shape, or form match the
world's standards. As a matter of fact, God's standards
and expectations contradict and challenge the commonly
accepted values and standards of the world. They turn the
world's standards upside down and inside out. When we are

wronged or hurt, God expects us to forgive; the world wants revenge. The world values accruing money and possessions and holding on to them; God smiles when we give them to those in need. The world expects us to love the people who love us; God expects us to love our enemies, including those who persecute us. Therefore, those of us who choose to follow Jesus are *in* the world though not *of* the world because we live our lives according to an entirely different set of standards and beliefs. Jesus underscored this point when he stood before the Roman governor, Pontius Pilate. Pilate asked him, "Are you the king of the Jews?" (John 18:33). Jesus answered, "My Kingdom is not an earthly kingdom. . . . My Kingdom is not of this world" (John 18:36). I don't know how he could have stated any clearer than this that though he was *in* the world, he was not *of* the world.

Just as Jesus was in the world but not of the world, his church is also to be in the world though not of the world. His church is not supposed to be a reflection of the world, it is supposed to stand apart so it can light up the world.

In regard to the status of women, the church became a reflection of the world when it constructed a stained glass ceiling which mirrored the glass ceiling in the world.

For those of you who are not familiar with the concept of the glass ceiling, "The glass ceiling metaphor has often been used to describe invisible barriers ('glass') through which women can see elite positions but cannot reach them ('ceiling'). These barriers prevent large numbers of women and ethnic minorities from obtaining and securing the most powerful, prestigious, and highest-grossing jobs in the workforce."

The stained glass ceiling, according to Wikipedia, is "a sociological phenomenon in religious communities similar to the concept of the glass ceiling. This concept revolves around the apparent difficulty for women who seek to gain a role within church leadership. The use of the term stained glass ceiling is metaphorical, indicating a certain level of power or authority within church structures that women tend not to rise above within church hierarchies."

## The pattern is disrupted

What is really sad and ironic is that church leaders constructed the stained glass ceiling with Paul's words, or rather, what they *thought* were Paul's words.

*Question:* If Jesus saw women as equal to men, and Paul saw women as equal to men, what happened that disrupted the pattern?

*Answer:* The disruption in the pattern occurred because the men who translated Paul's letters interpreted Paul's words through their lens of viewing reality. Their lens impacted the choice of English words to use in the translation. This led to discrepancies between the Greek words Paul used in his letters and the English words that were used in the translation of his letters. This then caused a distortion of Paul's message.

Each of us view reality through a lens comprised of values and beliefs about ourselves and our world. This lens colors what we see, and determines what we think about what we see. The values and beliefs which comprise our lens have their roots in what we were taught and what we experienced in the family and culture we grew up in. It was no different for the men who translated Paul's letters.

## The Translators' Lens

The beliefs regarding women that the translators of Paul's letters held were those of Gentile converts to the Christian faith. These beliefs had their roots in the Greek philosophy that was developed by the philosophers and teachers of Athens, the capital city of ancient Greece.

The first Greek philosopher to put into words that women were the weaker sex and inferior to men was Socrates. He lived from 470 to 399 BC. "The teachings of Socrates came down to us through his star pupil, Plato (427–347 BC). And Plato's most distinguished disciple was Aristotle (384–322 BC)."[31] In one of his writings, Aristotle stated, "The 'equality of the two or rule of the inferior is always hurtful.'"[32]

> Aristotle thus laid a lasting philosophical foundation for the notion that females are inferior to males. He formalized the practice of sexual discrimination and offered learned authority to the belief in sexual inequality. Centuries later, church leaders who themselves were a product of Greek culture and education interpreted Paul's writings from the perspective of Aristotelian philosophy.[33]

For example, Aristotle described a husband as the soul and his wife as the body; therefore, he argued, a husband is to rule his wife and a wife to obey her husband. So, when Paul wrote in his letter to the church in Ephesus, "For a husband is the head of his wife as Christ is the head of the church" (Ephesians 5:23), the men who were translating his letters assumed he was simply reiterating Aristotle's statement, when in fact he was challenging Aristotle's idea instead of agreeing with it.

John Temple Bristow, in his book *What Paul Really Said About Women*, describes clearly and definitively how this happened.

> Paul wrote in a dialect of the Greek language called koine . . . [the] most widely spoken and written language of Paul's time, understood by more people across the ancient world than any other.[34] . . . Words that Paul chose to use imply different ideas from those conveyed by the English words we use to translate his writings. . . . Our English words imply ideas that Paul deliberately avoided! If Paul had wanted to say what we think he said, then he would have chosen quite different words when he wrote. . . . Paul carefully chose his words, deliberately avoiding those Greek terms that, if he had used them, would have communicated to his readers precisely what our English translations imply for us today.[35]

In English, the word head means literally the physical head on one's body and figuratively the leader of a body of people. The two meanings are intertwined. Not so in Greek, where two different and distinct words are translated "head." One of these is *arche*. It means "head" in terms of leadership and point of origin. . . . *Arche* was also used to denote "first" in terms of importance and power. . . . Paul did not choose to use the word *arche* when he wrote of how the husband is head of his wife. He was well aware of that word, but he deliberately chose a different term. Instead, Paul used the word *kephale*. . . . It was never used to mean "leader" or "boss" or "chief" or "ruler." *Kephale* . . . means "one who leads," but not in the sense of "director." . . . A *kephale* was one who went before the troops, the leader in the sense of being in the lead, the first one into battle. . . . Paul was certainly familiar with both words. . . . The difference between the two would have been obvious to him. Modern readers, however, may misunderstand Paul, assuming that the word for head that Paul used also carried the figurative meaning of "boss" or "ruler." Paul in fact took great care not to say that.[36]

Rather than saying that a husband is to rule over his wife, Paul was saying that a husband is to nourish and sanctify his wife and even be willing to die for her, as Christ died for the church. Paul's analogy of the husband being the head of his wife as Christ is the head of the church, means being a servant of all, being willing to give up life itself for the body.

Gilbert Bilezikian, in his book *Beyond Sex Roles*, states, "The word head . . . conveys . . . the idea of provider, origin, starting point, and nurture. The concept might be better served in translation by the expression servant-provider or life-giver."[37]

## Point of View

Paul's words which have been used down through the ages to keep women out of pulpits and leadership roles in the church will be discussed from the point of view Sarah Sumner espouses in her book *Men and Women in the Church*: "Every reader of the Bible is faced with the challenge of discerning which passages in the text were originally intended to apply to believers of all ages and which ones were intended to apply only to the audience the writer addressed at the time."[38]

J. Lee Grady says something very similar in his book *10 Lies the Church Tells Women*. "Many parts of Scripture, of course, are to be applied universally. But in Paul's epistles, often his instructions are offered to bring correction to specific situations that had arisen in the early church."[39]

## Paul's Words

A Scripture passage of Paul's that has been used extensively to keep women out of pulpits and leadership roles in the church is 1 Corinthians 14:34: "Women should be silent during church meetings. It is not proper for them to speak." In order to accurately understand what Paul said here, his choice of Greek words and the English words chosen to translate his words need to be closely looked at, as well as the audience he was writing to and why he was writing to them.

Paul planted the church in Corinth during his first missionary journey and lived there for about one and a half years. After he left the Corinthian church, members of the church forgot parts of his teachings and distorted other parts. As a result, a number of serious problems developed in the congregation. In his two letters to them, Paul addressed these problems and attempted to bring correction.

One of these problems was misconduct in worship. Apparently, the worship services in the Corinthian church during this time were chaotic, with many people speaking simultaneously. Paul was trying to bring order and honor to the worship services.

> There is a word in Greek that means "tie shut," "muzzle." It is often used to describe a kind of forced silence. . . . This word is *phimoo*. . . . When Paul wrote that women are to be silent, he did not use *phimoo*, even though the English translation might imply such a forceful command. . . .
>
> Instead, Paul chose the Greek verb *sigao*. . . . *Sigao* is a voluntary silence. . . . *Sigao* is the kind of silence asked for in the midst of disorder and clamor. And Paul asked women of the church to keep that kind of silence.[40]

As to the second sentence in this verse admonishing women not to speak in church services:

> Greek has many words that can be translated "speak." Five of them denote preaching or proclaiming, and twenty-five others can be translated "say," "speak," or "teach." ...
>
> Paul wrote that women are not to *laleo.* Like the other verbs, *laleo* can denote the act of saying something quite important. But of all the verbs that can be translated "speak," only *laleo* can also mean, simply, "talk."[41]

Paul was simply asking the women not to talk, like students are asked not to talk in class.

> Paul's words about silence are simply calling for teachableness in his new female followers. Because women had not been trained to understand the Scriptures (in fact, they had been denied this opportunity!), he was calling them to embrace the discipline of learning the Word of God. ...
>
> Paul was calling women to listen and to learn. He was not telling them to shut up and be invisible. He was inviting them to enroll in the seminary of the Holy Spirit and to become active followers of Christ. ... And if Paul was calling women to learn, then he fully expected them to teach and preach what

they had been taught when the process of discipleship was complete.[42]

Another Scripture verse of Paul's that has been used down through the ages to keep women out of pulpits and leadership roles in the church is 1 Timothy 2:12: "I do not let women teach men or have authority over them. Let them listen quietly." Again, one has to look at the words Paul used and who he was writing to as well as why he was writing.

Paul was writing to his beloved disciple Timothy who at that time was serving as pastor of the church in Ephesus. Paul had planted that church and led it for three years. When Paul moved on in his apostolic journey he left his protégé, Timothy, to pastor the Ephesian church. This was a very difficult and challenging assignment for Timothy for two reasons. First, Timothy was young and was rather timid and unsure of himself. Second, this congregation was experiencing an influx of many false teachers (primarily women) who were preaching a distorted gospel which was, in essence, tearing the church apart. Timothy was charged with restoring order to the church and insuring that the true gospel was being taught. Paul wrote two letters to Timothy for the purpose of encouraging him and instructing him in this most difficult assignment.

Bible scholars have documented the fact that bizarre gnostic heresies were circulating throughout the region at that time, and these false teachings posed a serious threat to the infant Christian churches that were budding in that part of the world. . . .

Women were doing the teaching of these strange doctrines, at least in part. A major purpose of this entire epistle was to correct unbiblical teachings being presented by women.

. . . Certain cultic worship practices involving female priestesses of the Greek fertility goddess, Diana, had invaded the church of that day. These women priests promoted blasphemous ideas about sex and spirituality, and they sometimes actually performed rituals in which they pronounced curses on men in an attempt to spiritually emasculate them or to declare female superiority.

This teaching most certainly bred unhealthy attitudes among some women in the Ephesian church. These women were completely unlearned, but they were spreading false doctrines, and in some cases they were claiming to be teachers of the Law and demanding an audience. They were most likely mixing Christian and Jewish teachings with strange heresies and warped versions of Bible stories. . . .

Some of these rebellious women were actually disrupting worship services so they could teach their strange gospels. Rather than listening to church leaders who had been trained by Paul and the other apostles, these women were pridefully claiming that they deserved the pulpit themselves. . . .

Paul had to bring serious discipline to the situation quickly or the church would have been infected with a deadly virus. So he forbade these domineering women teachers from spreading their lies, and he commanded all the women in the congregation to be submissive so they could learn correct doctrine. The seriousness of the problem demanded a severe response.[43]

Paul brings a decisive solution to this problem: while they are still in the learning stage, those women should not attempt to become teachers or aspire to teach their own male teachers. Scholars have already noted that the present tense of Paul's "I do not permit" has the force of "I do not permit *now* a woman to teach." Presently, these women would have to learn by sitting quietly and receptively under authorized teachers. Then, when they continue in faith, love, sanctification, and discretion, there would remain no hindrance for them to serve as teachers, just as other women served as prophets in other churches.[44]

As to the words that Paul chose to use when forbidding women to teach men and have authority over men, he used the word *authenteo*. This word "appears nowhere else in the New Testament. . . . It was used to indicate how one may act on his or her own authority, and dominate others in an autocratic way. 'Domineer' may be a good translation of *authenteo*."[45] When Paul said that women were to "listen quietly," he used the word *hesuchia*. "It does not mean simply refraining from talking. It means restful quietness, as in meditation or study."[46] It differs from the word *sigao* which means "being quiet in order to hear someone speak" and *hesuchia* is "being quiet in order to listen with studious attention."[47]

> This tendency to interpret Scripture from the viewpoint of Greek philosophy was finally given highest expression in the thirteenth century in the writings of Thomas Aquinas . . . . Aquinas did more than any other to systematize Christian beliefs and to harmonize them with Greek philosophy. . . . Aquinas interpreted the writings of Saint Paul through the mind of Aristotle, and the Greek deprecation of women became solidly infused within Christian theology.[48]

If church leaders are to begin to view women through God's eyes and follow the example set by Jesus and Paul and other early church leaders in allowing and encouraging women to serve in all levels and roles in ministry, many people are going to have to swim upstream and many boats will have to be rocked.

Another way to influence change is to throw a stone in a pond. So, if you're not ready to swim upstream, try throwing a stone in a pond.

# CHAPTER EIGHT

# THE RIPPLE EFFECT

When you throw a stone in a pond, circular ripples go out from the stone in all directions. The thrower does not know how far the ripples will go or what they might touch along the way. I imagine Rosa Parks had no idea what the ripple effect would be when she refused to give up her seat on a bus in Montgomery, Alabama, on December 1, 1955.

## A Stone in Montgomery

The Montgomery City Code required that all public transportation be segregated. While operating a bus, drivers were required to provide separate but equal accommodations for white and black passengers by assigning seats. They did this by marking a line roughly in the middle of the bus, separating white passengers in the front of the bus from black passengers in the back.

When a black passenger boarded the bus, he or she had to get on at the front to pay the fare, then get off and reboard the bus through the back door. When the seats in the front of the bus filled up and more white passengers got on, the bus driver would move the sign back separating black and white passengers and, if necessary, ask black passengers to give up their seats. Though the city's bus ordinance did give drivers the authority to assign seats, it did not specifically give them the authority to demand passengers give up a seat to anyone (regardless of color). However, Montgomery bus drivers had adopted the custom of telling black passengers to give their seats to white passengers, when no other seats were available. If a black passenger protested, the bus driver had the authority to stop the bus and call the police to have him or her removed from the bus.

On December 1, 1955, after a long day's work as a seamstress in a department store, Rosa Parks boarded the Cleveland Avenue bus for home. She took a seat in the first of several rows designated for "colored" passengers. As the bus began to fill with white passengers, the driver noticed that several white passengers were standing in the aisle. He stopped the bus and moved the sign separating the two sections. He then told four black passengers to give their seats to white passengers. Three of the four passengers complied, Rosa did not. The bus driver called the police. They arrested Rosa at the scene and charged her with violation of chapter 6, section 11, of the Montgomery City Code. She was released on bail later that night.

On the evening Rosa Parks was arrested, E. D. Nixon, head of the local chapter of the National Association for the Advancement of Colored People (NAACP), decided to organize a boycott of Montgomery's city buses in protest of Rosa's arrest. Ads were placed in local newspapers and flyers were printed and distributed in black neighborhoods. The flyers read:

Another woman has been arrested and thrown in jail because she refused to get up out of her seat on the bus for a white person to sit down. It is the second time since the Claudette Colvin case that a Negro woman has been arrested for the same thing. This has to be stopped. Negroes have rights too, for if Negroes did not ride the buses, they could not operate. Three-fourths of the riders are Negro, yet we are arrested, or have to stand over empty seats. If we do not do something to stop these arrests, they will continue. The next time it may be you, or your daughter, or mother. This woman's case will come up on Monday. We are, therefore, asking every Negro to stay off the buses Monday in protest of the arrest and trial. Don't ride the buses to work, to town, to school, or anywhere on Monday. You can afford to stay out of school for one day if you have no other way to go except by bus. You can also afford to stay out of town for one day. If you work, take a cab, or walk. But please, children and grown-ups, don't ride the bus at all on Monday. Please stay off all buses Monday. (Wikipedia)

Black ministers announced the boycott in church on Sunday, December 4, and the Montgomery Advertiser, a general-interest newspaper, published a front-page article on the planned action.

On December 5, Rosa was found guilty of violating a local ordinance and was fined $10, as well as a $4 court fee, and most of the estimated forty thousand black commuters living in the city at the time boycotted the buses. Many opted to walk to work that day—some as far as twenty miles. The city's buses were, for the most part, empty.

As the boycott was such a huge success, civil rights leaders in Montgomery decided to continue it. On the afternoon of December 5, they met to discuss strategy. They decided that their boycott effort required a new organization and strong leadership. They formed the Montgomery Improvement Association and elected the twenty-six-year-old pastor of Montgomery's Dexter Avenue Baptist Church, Dr. Martin Luther King Jr., as their leader.

The black population of the city supported the boycott with unequivocal cooperation. Dozens of public buses sat idle for months. As the boycott continued, segregationists retaliated with violence. Black churches were burned, and both Martin Luther King Jr.'s home and E. D. Nixon's home were destroyed by bombings. In addition, black citizens were arrested for violating an antiquated law prohibiting boycotts.

In response to these events, the black community initiated legal action. Armed with the *Brown v. Board of Education* decision, which stated that separate but equal policies had no place in public education, a black legal team took the issue of segregation on public transit systems to the US District Court for the Middle District of Alabama, Northern (Montgomery) Division. The suit was heard in June 1956 and the court ruled that Alabama's racial segregation laws for buses were unconstitutional. The State of Alabama appealed the decision. The boycott continued. The case moved on to the United States Supreme Court. The boycott continued throughout this process. On November 13, 1956, the Supreme Court upheld the district court's ruling and ordered the state to desegregate the buses.

The boycott officially ended on December 20, 1956. It had lasted 381 days. The city of Montgomery passed an ordinance authorizing black bus passengers to sit virtually anywhere they chose on buses.

Though the Montgomery Bus Boycott proved to be one of the largest and most successful acts of civil disobedience in the civil rights struggle, both Rosa Parks and her husband experienced very unpleasant consequences because of it. They both lost their jobs and she received death threats for years. Unable to find work, they eventually left Montgomery and moved to Detroit, Michigan. Rosa lived there until her death at age ninety-two on October 24, 2005.

After the Montgomery Bus Boycott Martin Luther King Jr. became the de facto leader of the civil rights movement. He went on to throw many stones in many ponds, causing amazing ripples to fan out in many directions. These led to significant victories in the civil rights struggle. Some of the stones were thrown in the Selma, Alabama, pond.

## Stones in Selma

Following the passage of the Civil Rights Act of 1964, Martin Luther King Jr. told President Lyndon Johnson that a voting rights act was needed in order for black Americans to truly impact their communities. Johnson told King that it would be five to ten years before that law could be passed.

King, however, was committed to swimming upstream in order to obtain full civil rights for black people in the United States as soon as possible. He was not willing to tread water for five to ten years. That's when he, as well as other leaders of the Southern Christian Leadership Conference (SCLC), began to throw stones in the Selma, Alabama, pond.

On March 7, 1965, leaders of the SCLC marched across the Edmond Pettus Bridge alongside the people of Selma, (approximately 600 people in all) to face the notorious Sheriff Jim Clark and his virtual army of angry white policemen. One young marcher, John Lewis, was beaten almost to death by the police, and many others were injured and/or arrested. This day came to be called Bloody Sunday.

Two weeks later, in response to that brutal event, hundreds of clergy representing many denominations from all over the country, arrived in Selma to join a Selma to Montgomery march. On Sunday, March 21, about thirty-two hundred marchers left Selma and set out for Montgomery. They walked twelve miles a day and slept in fields. Others joined them all along the way. By the time they reached Montgomery on Thursday, March 25, there were approximately twenty-five thousand marchers.

Five months later the Voting Rights Act of 1965 was passed. This law removed legal barriers at state and local levels which had been stopping black men from exercising the right to vote which had been given to them in 1870 with the passage of the Fifteenth Amendment to the Constitution. The Voting Rights Act also specifically gave black women the right to vote.

Both Martin Luther King Jr. and Rosa Parks were present on August 6, 1965, when Lyndon Johnson signed the Voting Rights Act into law.

*Worthwhile Information to Know:* Martin Luther King Jr. led the Civil Rights Movement until his assassination on April 4, 1968. Over the course of those twelve and a half years he was arrested thirty times. All the arrests were for misdemeanor offenses related to nonviolent civil rights protests in which he participated. Some of his arrests resulted in jail time and some resulted in fines.

# CHAPTER NINE

# A HEALTHY BODY

Before he was crucified Jesus planted the church so his work could continue throughout time. He meant for the church to be his hands, feet, and heart in the world—his body. The apostle Paul wrote about this in his letter to the church in Ephesus. "God has put all things under the authority of Christ and has made him head over all things for the benefit of the church. And the church is his body" (Ephesians 1:22–23). "We will speak the truth in love, growing in every way more and more like Christ, who is the head of his body, the church" (Ephesians 4:15).

If a church body is to effectively carry on Jesus's work in the world, it needs to be healthy. Any body, for that matter, needs to be healthy if it is to function properly and fulfill the purpose for which it was created. The body of Christ is no exception. If a church body is not healthy, it is doubtful that this body will be able to effectively fulfill the purpose for which it was planted—to be a bright, shining light in the world.

In his letter to the church in Corinth, the apostle Paul educated them as to how to be a healthy body of Christ.

The human body has many parts, but the many parts make up one whole body. So it is with the body of Christ. . . . Yes, the body has many different parts, not just one part. If the foot says, "I am not a part of the body because I am not a hand," that does not make it any less a part of the body. And if the ear says, "I am not part of the body because I am not an eye," would that make it any less a part of the body? If the whole body were an eye, how would you hear? Or if your whole body were an ear, how would you smell anything?

But our bodies have many parts, and God has put each part just where he wants it. How strange a body would be if it had only one part! Yes, there are many parts, but only one body. (1 Corinthians 12:12, 14–20)

*Question:* So, in a healthy body of Christ, how do you determine who is a hand and who is a foot and who is an ear?

*Answer:* By discerning what spiritual gifts an individual has been given.

## Spiritual Gifts

When an individual gives his or her life to God, that individual becomes part of God's family. The Holy Spirit then comes to live inside that believer and endows him or her with spiritual gifts. A spiritual gift is an ability or talent that is given to an individual by God when he or she becomes part of God's family. Though each believer receives spiritual gifts, not everyone receives the same gifts. Individuals are given spiritual gifts to equip them for the purpose God chose for them and designed them to fulfill. Paul explained this to the church in Corinth when he said:

> A spiritual gift is given to each of us so we can help each other. To one person the Spirit gives the ability to give wise advice; to another the same Spirit gives a message of special knowledge. The same Spirit gives great faith to another, and to someone else the one Spirit gives the gift of healing. He gives one person the power to perform miracles, and another the ability to prophesy. He gives someone else the ability to discern whether a message is from the Spirit of God or from another spirit. Still another person is given the ability to speak in unknown languages, while another is given the ability to interpret what is being said. It is the one and only Spirit who distributes all these gifts. He alone decides which gift each person should have. (1 Corinthians 12:7–11)

Paul then went on to stress that all spiritual gifts are necessary and needed in the body of Christ. He makes the point that if the body is to be healthy and function effectively, all parts must do what they were meant to do. The body won't be able to function if an ear tries to see and an eye tries to hear. In addition, he clearly states that no parts are more important than any other. "The eye can never say to the hand, 'I don't need you.' The head can't say to the feet, 'I don't need you.' . . . All of you together are Christ's body, and each of you is a part of it" (1 Corinthians 12:21, 27).

Paul also discussed spiritual gifts in his letter to the church in Rome (Romans 12) and his letter to the church in Ephesus (Ephesians 4).

*Important Point:* There is no reference in any of Paul's letters to gifts being distributed according to gender. Also, in the account of the events which occurred on the day of Pentecost, the book of Acts clearly states that everyone present was filled with the Holy Spirit.

> On the day of Pentecost all the believers were meeting together in one place. Suddenly, there was a sound from heaven like the roaring of a mighty windstorm, and it filled the house where they were sitting. Then, what looked like flames or tongues of fire appeared and settled on each of them. And everyone present was filled with the Holy Spirit. (Acts 2:1–4)

Since only a few brief verses before this, Scripture tells us that they all (including the women) met together and were constantly united in prayer, there is nothing to indicate that the women were not present when the Holy Spirit came. It does not say that the men were filled with the Holy Spirit. It says that *everyone* was filled with the Holy Spirit. There is also nothing to indicate that the women were not endowed with spiritual gifts.

*Question:* Where do women belong in the twenty-first-century church?

*Answer:* Wherever God places them.

God has carved out places for every one of his daughters in his church, and he wants us to occupy the places he chose for us. Whatever spiritual gift or gifts you were given, you were given for a reason and a purpose, and he wants you to use it for the purpose he chose for you. He does not want you to hide it. If you choose to hide your gift(s), God is displeased. In his book *The Purpose Driven Life* Rick Warren states, "You don't bring glory or pleasure to God by hiding your abilities or by trying to be someone else. You only bring him enjoyment by being you. Anytime you reject any part of yourself, you are rejecting God's wisdom and sovereignty in creating you."[49]

## God has a plan

The concept of God having a plan and a purpose for everyone he creates is referenced throughout the Bible. Isaiah, an Old Testament prophet, told Cyrus, a pagan king, about God's purposes and plans for him. He then said, in God's name, "And why have I called you for this work? Why did I call you by name when you did not know me? It is for the sake of Jacob my servant, Israel my chosen one. I am the LORD; there is no other God. I have equipped you for battle, though you don't even know me" (Isaiah 45:4–5).

The people of Israel then began to question God for working through a pagan king. To them, Isaiah said,

"Does a clay pot argue with its maker? Does the clay dispute with the one who shapes it, saying 'Stop, you're doing it wrong!' Does the pot exclaim, 'How clumsy can you be!' How terrible it would be if a newborn baby said to its father, 'Why was I born?' Or if it said to its mother, 'Why did you make me this way?'" This is what the LORD says—the Holy One of Israel and your Creator: "Do you question what I do for my children? Do you give me orders about the work of my hands? I am the one who made the earth and created people to live on it. With my hands I stretched out the heavens. All the stars are at my command. I will raise up Cyrus to fulfill my righteous purpose, and I will guide his actions." (Isaiah 45:9–13)

Isaiah is telling the people of Israel in no uncertain terms that God is sovereign, that he knows what he is doing, and that he chooses whomever he wants to do whatever he wants.

*Newsflash:* God does not make mistakes. Human beings make mistakes.

As stated above, God put each of us on earth to fulfill a specific purpose that he chose especially for us. He designed us to fulfill that purpose by giving us the spiritual gifts we would need to fulfill it. Another way of saying this is that God anoints each of us to do the work he wants us to do, *and* he wired us to succeed.

## Ordination vs. Anointing

God anoints. Human beings ordain.

When God anoints someone to do something it is very different than someone deciding to go into professional ministry and being given the seal of approval, or being ordained, by human beings to do that work.

Wikipedia defines ordination as "the process by which individuals are consecrated, that is, set apart as clergy to perform various religious rites and ceremonies." Inherent in this definition is the understanding that it is human beings who are doing the consecrating. The difference between ordination and anointing is that God is at the center of the anointing process and human beings are at the center of the ordination process. In the Maxwell Leadership Bible, John Maxwell defines anointing as "God's intimate presence and enabling power."

It is important to understand that someone can be ordained by human beings to do something and not be anointed by God to do that same thing. It is also possible that someone can be anointed by God to do something and not have the approval or blessing of human beings to do that.

An obvious question would then be: How can you tell if an individual has been anointed by God to fill a particular ministry role? Bill Hybels, John Maxwell, and Joyce Meyer helped me answer that question. Before I outline the answer I came up with through their combined wisdom though, there is one important point I would like to highlight. That is, it is important to remember that though someone may be anointed by God to fill a ministry role, that individual is still human and, therefore, not perfect. He or she will make mistakes and will have flaws. The mistakes and the flaws do not cancel out the divine anointing, and the anointing does not remove all traces of an imperfect human nature. So, how do you tell if someone is anointed by God?

Indicators of a divine anointing are:

- determination,

- focus,

- internal motivation,

- all-consuming vision, and

- contagious passion.

The determination of someone who is anointed by God to do something is an absolute refusal to give up. Joyce Meyer, in her book *A Leader in the Making*, describes it as a "holy determination" to "press on until we see the fulfillment of God's plan for our life."[50]

The focus exhibited by someone who is anointed by God is like a laser. Rick Warren describes this very eloquently in *The Purpose Driven Life*: "Diffused light has little power or impact, but you can concentrate its energy by focusing it. With a magnifying glass, the rays of the sun can be focused to set grass or paper on fire. When light is focused even more as a laser beam, it can cut through steel."[51]

Internal motivation can also be described as self-discipline. Someone who is internally motivated does not need anyone else to tell them what to do or when to do it.

The impetus for action comes from inside them. It comes from the vision God has given them for their life purpose and the passion that vision evokes in them.

Bill Hybels defines vision as "a picture of the future that produces passion."[52]

Merriam-Webster Dictionary defines passion as "a strong feeling of enthusiasm or excitement for something or about doing something."

In summary, in my opinion, if a church body is to effectively carry on Jesus's work in the world it needs to be healthy. In order for it to be healthy, it needs to be devoid of "isms." When church leaders are making decisions regarding who is to fill what ministry role, the leaders need to be color-blind and gender-blind, seeing individuals as equal—different yet equal. I strongly believe that these decisions need to be based on spiritual gifts and calling alone. Gender and race have no part in these decisions.

# CHAPTER TEN

# SWIMMING UPSTREAM

When an individual first begins to swim upstream against the status quo, it is not unusual for him or her to initially swim alone. If the swimmer perseveres, however, often other swimmers will eventually join him or her.

When Elizabeth Stanton first began to advocate for women's rights, her father and husband did not support her women's rights work. Rather than letting this stop her, however, she went underground, writing newspaper articles and letters to the editor under the pen name of Sunflower. As discussed in chapter two, Susan B. Anthony and other women eventually joined her, and they formed a strong and formidable alliance. Together they laid a firm foundation for the movement which eventually earned women the right to vote and then further down the road secured other rights for women.

Another Elizabeth, Elizabeth Blackwell, swam upstream in the male dominated medical field in the nineteenth century. She was the first woman to receive a medical degree in the United States. She then paved the way for other women to earn medical degrees.

## Elizabeth's Story

Elizabeth Blackwell was born in England in 1821. Her family moved to America when she was eleven. Upon reaching adulthood she went into teaching, as that was considered an appropriate profession for a woman. About one year into her teaching career a close friend of hers who was dying told Elizabeth that she believed she would have been spared her worst suffering if her doctor had been a woman. This event resulted in Elizabeth switching her career to medicine.

Elizabeth's first step in her career change was to move to Philadelphia because Philadelphia was considered to be the center of medical learning in America. She applied for admission to the four medical schools there. She was rejected by all of them. A professor at the largest medical school told her she could enter if she disguised herself as a man. Another professor advised her to go to Paris for medical training. She refused to do either one.

She then applied to twelve more medical schools in the Northeast. She was finally accepted at Geneva Medical College in upstate New York in 1847. It was not the faculty of Geneva, however, who decided to accept her. It was the students. The faculty, assuming that the all-male student body would never agree to a woman joining their ranks, put the question of Elizabeth's acceptance to a vote. The students voted yes, and Elizabeth became the first woman in the United States to gain admittance to a medical school.

She graduated with her medical degree in 1849. With the help of friends, she opened the New York Infirmary for Women and Children in 1857. In addition to providing medical care for the poor, this institution provided internships for female medical students. By doing this, Elizabeth removed one of the obstacles female medical students encountered—medical institutions refusing to accept them for internships. She also published several important books on the issue of women in medicine, including *Medicine as a Profession for Women* in 1860 and *Address on the Medical Education of Women* in 1864.

She retired from medical practice in the late 1870s due to declining health.

The medical profession was not the only profession in which women had to swim upstream to gain access. The legal field was also a very difficult arena for women to enter. Many obstacles were thrown in their way to stop them from entering this male dominated profession.

## Cracking the Legal Field's Glass Ceiling

In the nineteenth century, one did not necessarily need to attend law school to become a lawyer. Individuals who wanted to become lawyers could apprentice with an established lawyer. In return for paying the lawyer a fee, the individual would receive academic instruction from the lawyer as well as practical experience working in the lawyer's office. The individual could not practice on his own, however, until he passed the bar exam and was admitted to the bar in his state of residence. Admission to the bar typically followed reading law in a lawyer's office and demonstrating competence and character.

Arabella Mansfield was one of the first, if not the first, female lawyer in the United States. Arabella "read the law" as an apprentice in her brother's law office in Iowa. Despite an Iowa state law restricting the bar exam to males, Arabella took the exam and did very well. She challenged the law in court and Iowa changed its licensing statute, becoming the first state to accept women and minorities into its bar. She was admitted to the Iowa bar in 1869. She never actually practiced law, however, she chose instead to work as a college educator and administrator.

Ada Kepley graduated from Union College of Law in Chicago (now Northwestern) in 1870. She was denied a license to practice law in Illinois because of her gender. She therefore never officially became a lawyer. The Illinois law forbidding women to be practicing lawyers was overturned in 1881.

Charlotte E. Ray was the first African-American woman lawyer. She graduated from Howard University and was admitted to the District of Columbia bar in 1872. She experienced no difficulty getting admitted to the bar because she applied for admission under the name C. E. Ray and the admissions committee assumed she was a man.

Belva Lockwood attended National University in Washington, DC (now George Washington University), earning a law degree in 1873. She was admitted to the District of Columbia bar after overcoming stiff opposition and, in 1879, became the first woman in American history to argue a case before the Supreme Court.

## Sisters in Law

Two twentieth-century women (Sandra Day O'Connor and Ruth Bader Ginsburg) not only successfully removed every obstacle put in their paths to becoming practicing lawyers, they eventually were able to use the positions they attained to make women legally equal to men. Sandra Day O'Connor was the first woman to be appointed to the United States Supreme Court. Ruth Bader Ginsburg was the second. They swam upstream long and hard against intense opposition to make women equal to men in the eyes of the law.

## Sandra's Journey

Sandra attended Stanford Law School where she received her law degree in 1952. After graduating from law school she experienced great difficulty obtaining a position as an attorney. At least forty law firms refused to interview her for a position as an attorney because she was a woman. She eventually found employment as a deputy county attorney in San Mateo, California. She was hired because she agreed to work for no salary and without an office, sharing space with a secretary.

She went on to serve as Assistant Attorney General of Arizona from 1965 to 1969. She was then appointed to fill a vacancy in the Arizona State Senate. She was elected to the state senate in 1973 and became the first woman to serve as its majority leader. In 1974 she was elected to the Maricopa County Superior Court, serving from 1975 to 1979. She was then promoted to the Arizona State Court of Appeals where she served until she was nominated for the Supreme Court by President Ronald Reagan in 1981.

## Ruth's Journey

Ruth enrolled at Harvard Law School in 1956. She was one of nine women in a class of about five hundred. Harvard's gender hierarchy became blatantly clear to her when she discovered that the sole ladies' restroom was in the basement of one of the two classroom buildings. The message about the gender hierarchy at Harvard was loudly reinforced (as if it needed to be) when Erwin Griswold, Dean of Harvard Law, asked Ruth and the other female law students, "How do you justify taking a spot from a qualified man?" Ruth's reply to him was, "It's important for wives to understand their husband's work."

She completed her first two years of law school at Harvard then transferred to Columbia Law School when her husband took a job in New York City. She did her third year at Columbia where she earned her law degree in 1959.

Like Sandra, Ruth found it very difficult to secure a position as a lawyer upon graduation. In 1960, she became a clerk for a judge in the US District Court for the Southern District of New York, a position she held for two years. In 1963 she moved into the position of law professor at Rutgers Law School in New Jersey. When she accepted that position, she was informed she would be paid less than her male colleagues because she had a husband who had a good paying job. She left Rutgers in 1972 to teach at Columbia Law School, where she stayed until 1980.

In addition to teaching, she cofounded the Women's Rights Law Reporter in 1970, the first law journal in the United States to focus exclusively on women's rights. In 1972, she cofounded the Women's Rights Project at the

American Civil Liberties Union (ACLU), and in 1973, she became the ACLU's General Counsel.

President Jimmy Carter appointed Ruth to the US Court of Appeals for the District of Columbia Circuit in 1980. She served there for thirteen years, until President Bill Clinton nominated her for the Supreme Court in 1993.

## The Women's Movement

"Right after women won the vote in 1920, the most radical of the suffrage leaders, Alice Paul, proposed an Equal Rights Amendment for women as the only way to attack the whole web of discriminatory laws at once. Despite Paul's half century of effort, the ERA had gone nowhere."[53] Then, in the early 1960s, women all over the country began to swim upstream against the injustice of gender inequality and "the earthquake we call the feminist movement"[54] erupted.

"The new movement revived the old call for an amendment to the Constitution, the Equal Rights Amendment, protecting women, just as the Civil War amendments protected black Americans."[55]

Sandra Day O'Connor and Ruth Bader Ginsburg "chose to become lawyers when there was not even a whisper of a women's legal movement, but their choice of career placed them perfectly to make a social revolution through the law when the opportunity arose."[56]

Ruth's "first act of feminist insurgency was to visit the [Rutgers Law] library and gather all the materials there were on the subject of Women and the Law."[57] "When Ginsburg left the Rutgers library, she had learned that laws excluded women from countless human activities. Women could not or need not serve on juries, and, therefore, they would never

111

be judged by juries of their peers. They could not tend bar in unhealthy saloons and so would-be barkeeps could not earn their keep." [58] Ruth's trip to the Rutgers library was the beginning of her uphill battle for gender equality. The time she spent in the library has been described as "consciousness raising" and "life altering" for her. From this point on, she was a tireless and fearless advocate for women's rights. She "turned her powerful analytic mind to the problem of using the equality language of the Constitution to destabilize the wall between men's and women's roles."[59] She, and the other women lawyers fighting alongside her, knew they "were going to have to fight trench warfare to extract legal equality from the existing, race-based constitutional provisions."[60] "The highest goal was obvious: get the court to see sex like race."[61]

One of the first actions she took in the early '70s was to write letters to each member of the Senate and House Judiciary Committees advocating for the passage of the Equal Rights Amendment. As of the time of this writing (2017) the Equal Rights Amendment has still not passed Congress and become the law of the land.

*Personal note:* Though it is incredibly sad to me that the ERA never passed Congress and became law, it is even sadder that a law needs to be in place for women and men to be treated as equals. To me, this is clear evidence that "isms" are still very much alive and well. In a perfect world it wouldn't matter what the law says because men and women would see each other as different yet equal, and it is this belief which would drive behavior, not a law. However, as we all know, we do not live in a perfect world.

While Ruth was fine-tuning her social conscience and setting a direction for her life in New York and New Jersey, Sandra was educating herself in Arizona regarding laws which perpetuated and reinforced gender discrimination. She was reading about the work women's rights activists were doing on both the west coast and the east coast, and compiling a list of laws at every level of government in the United States which treated women and men differently. One of the first actions she took, as a member of the Arizona State Senate, was to have the state law limiting women to an eight-hour work day repealed. It was believed that this law was a tool which was used to keep women out of jobs with more responsibility and influence, as well as higher pay. Though she faced stiff opposition as she worked to have this law repealed, she eventually succeeded and the law was overturned.

Sandra also led "a bi-partisan effort to repeal the web of Arizona laws that discriminated against women. She was visibly behind the revision of Arizona's community property law to allow women rights of management over marital property and to remove male-only language that sometimes carried a real sting, for instance, that only fathers could sue for the death or injury of a child."[62]

Sandra never became an ardent feminist like Ruth. Her opinions and decisions were not always aligned with women's rights/gender equality. She did, however, do much to advance the cause of gender equality. Her contribution was not only the equality legislation she fought for in the Arizona Senate, or later supported as a Supreme Court justice. Rather, her most powerful and lasting contribution was as a role model. She was not only the first woman to serve as a majority leader in the Arizona State Senate, she was the first woman to serve as a majority leader in *any* state senate and, as stated above, she was the first female justice on the United States Supreme Court. By serving in these positions she put serious cracks in these glass ceilings.

While Sandra was fighting trench warfare in the Arizona legislature, Ruth was the chief litigator for the Women's Rights Project of the American Civil Liberties Union (ACLU). As such, she wrote legal briefs and argued several landmark cases before the Supreme Court. She attained a reputation as a skilled oral advocate and her work directly led to the end of gender discrimination in many areas of the law, such as

- having a law repealed that forbid women to be executors of dead people's estates;

- overturning laws which forbid women to serve on juries;

- granting women in the armed forces the same housing and medical benefits for their spouses that servicemen automatically received (servicewomen had previously been denied these benefits); and

- granting husbands of working wives Social Security survivor benefits (prior to this, only women were eligible for this benefit).

Ruth ". . . never got the Supreme Court to say that sex was like race. However, . . . never again would the Supreme Court say that an American law could treat women differently from men simply because they were women."[63] Ruth ". . . had changed the law's presumptions about sex distinctions. In five short years, she had built a structure of women's equality . . ."[64]

## Sandra takes her seat

As stated above, Sandra was nominated for the Supreme Court by President Ronald Reagan in July, 1981. She was subsequently confirmed and sworn in on September 25, 1981.

A few weeks after she took her seat as a Supreme Court justice *Hogan v. Mississippi*, a sex discrimination case, came before the Court. The case began when Joe Hogan decided he wanted to study nursing at Mississippi University for Women, a public college near his home. He was denied admission due to his gender and sued. He won his case in his local court when Mississippi University for Women was ordered to admit men to its nursing school. The State of Mississippi appealed the decision.

When the case came before the Supreme Court, Sandra was the swing vote. Four justices voted to uphold the lower court's ruling and four justices voted to overturn it. Because of Sandra's vote, the state of Mississippi was ordered to admit both women *and* men to their public nursing schools.

Five years into O'Connor's tenure, the first women's affirmative action case, *Johnson v.*

*Santa Clara Transportation Authority*, came before the Court. The Transportation Authority had adopted an affirmative action plan allowing sex to be considered as a factor in promotion; shortly thereafter, it promoted the first woman in its history to the position of head dispatcher, lowering the ratio of men to women in that job category from 238:0 to 237:1. Johnson, a man who had scored two points higher than the woman promoted on the graded interview, filed a lawsuit, claiming the affirmative action was actually reverse discrimination, in violation of the Civil Rights Act.[65]

Six of the nine justices, including O'Connor, voted to approve the affirmative action. When Justice Brennan wrote the majority opinion, Sandra disagreed with part of it. "She wanted to allow employers to adopt affirmative action only as a remedy for past behavior so bad it amounted to a violation of the Civil Rights Act."[66]

"Brennan really did not want to require employers to confess to prior civil rights violations in order to defend a voluntary affirmative action program. What company would ever admit that?"[67] Brennan did not make this change and Sandra withdrew her support. "The majority simply required that the employer be trying to rectify a 'manifest imbalance' in the workplace."[68] "Thousands if not millions of women and racial minorities got jobs and educations, which would never have happened if the Court had struck down affirmative action as reverse discrimination per se."[69]

## A Ripple Effect

One of the ripple effects of the women's movement in the 1970s was that sexual harassment in the workplace began to come to light and was put under a legal microscope. In 1976 a sexual harassment case came before the District of Columbia Circuit Court and, for the first time, a court ruled in favor of a female employee. The woman, Paulette Barnes, had been approached by her male supervisor for sex. When she refused, she was fired. The ruling was that this was sex discrimination under the Civil Rights Act.

Another sex discrimination case, *Meritor Savings Bank v. Vinson*, surfaced soon after and made its way to the Supreme Court. Sidney Taylor, branch manager of a Baltimore bank, asked trainee teller, Mechelle Vinson, to go to a motel with him to have sex. She initially refused, however, eventually agreed out of fear of losing her job.

> Taylor thereafter made repeated demands upon her for sexual favors, usually at the branch, both during and after business hours; she estimated that over the next several years she had intercourse with him some forty or fifty times. In addition, respondent testified that Taylor fondled her in front of other employees, followed her into the women's restroom when she went there alone, exposed himself to her, and even forcibly raped her on several occasions. When Taylor fired Vinson, allegedly for unrelated reasons, she sued.[70]

She lost in her local court in February 1980. Two weeks later the Equal Employment Opportunity Commission declared that sexual harassment was illegal job discrimination. When her case reached the Supreme Court in 1986 the bank argued that even if these things had happened, she had not been fired or demoted due to anything to do with these events, so therefore she had no claim.

The Court voted unanimously that Mechelle had a legitimate case of sexual harassment, even if she had not gotten fired or been demoted because of it. "Harassment that creates a hostile work environment, unheard of ten years before, was now ensconced firmly in the prohibitions of the Civil Rights Act."[71]

The justices were divided, however, over who was liable for the harassment—the bank or the individual supervisor. Four justices thought the bank should be held accountable for the harassment and four justices voted to limit liability to the supervisor. Sandra again was the critical swing vote. She voted with the justices who held that liability was limited to the supervisor.

## Ruth Takes Her Seat

When Ruth joined Sandra on the Supreme Court bench in 1993, one of the first cases that came before the Court was a sexual harassment case, *Harris v. Forklift Systems*. Charles Hardy, company president, called a female manager, Teresa Harris, derogatory names and "asked her (and other female employees) to fish in his front pants pockets for coins, to pick up objects he threw on the ground, and to come down to the Holiday Inn to negotiate her raise."[72] He also asked her, in front of a customer, if she had offered this customer sex. She quit, then she sued.

The lower court ruled against her saying that Hardy's behavior was not bad enough to cause her serious emotional or psychological harm. The Supreme Court justices, however, decided unanimously that emotional and/or psychological damage was not necessary to determine sexual harassment. Sandra wrote the majority opinion. "Her cautious first draft only marginally reduced the standard for proving sexual harassment, suggesting the workplace must be abusive before a victim could sue."[73] Ruth wanted to add, "The standard for sexual harassment under the Civil Rights Act should be the same as the rule for race: Would the offending behavior make it harder for a reasonable person to do their job?"[74] Sandra refused to add this and Ruth decided not to contest her decision. "This exchange . . . set O'Connor's and Ginsburg's roles in the cause of women's equality. Sandra Day O'Connor played defense; she would not permit the courts to roll the equality ball backward. . . . Ruth Bader Ginsburg . . . played offense."[75]

"Five years later, the Court moved beyond O'Connor's cautious formulation and explicitly adopted Ginsburg's standard as the law of the land."[76]

In 1995 a very high profile gender equality case came before the Supreme Court, *United States v. Virginia*. This case began in 1989 when an anonymous woman was denied admission to the all-male Virginia Military Institute.

> The Justice Department concluded that Virginia's policy of excluding women from VMI

violated the Fourteenth Amendment, which guarantees to all persons the equal protection of the laws. The United States would force Virginia to comply with the Constitution.[77]

From the start of the case in 1989 until the Supreme Court ruled in 1996, the VMI community of alumni and friends was firmly committed to resisting the women. Although the state of Virginia ultimately resigned from defending its public university's exclusionary policy, VMI raised and spent $14 million defending itself against the United States.[78]

In the end, the Supreme Court overturned decisions that had been made by lower courts which supported VMI's policy of sex segregation. Ruth wrote and delivered the decision ordering VMI to admit women. "The next year a handful of young women appeared on the VMI campus, hair cropped and sporting hilariously ill-fitting uniform skirts."[79]

In 1998 another gender equality case came before the Supreme Court by a rather circuitous route—immigration. During the Vietnam War (1964–74) many American men fathered children with Vietnamese women and women from other Asian countries. "American citizenship law gave the fathers eighteen years to claim their offspring, in order to confer citizenship on them. American mothers of children born abroad to foreign fathers had no such duty. Their children's citizenship was assumed. The law discriminated."[80]

In the mid 1990s the twenty-year-old daughter of an American serviceman and Filipino woman tried to become an American citizen. Her father had not claimed her before her eighteenth birthday. When the case reached the Supreme Court in 1997 a majority of the justices voted to uphold the American citizenship law which was in place. Ruth dissented. In her dissenting opinion she stated,

> Even if one accepts at face value the Government's current rationale, it is surely based on generalizations (stereotypes) about the way women (or men) are. These generalizations pervade the opinion of Justice Stevens, which constantly relates and relies on what "typically" or "normally," or "probably" happens "often." We have repeatedly cautioned, however, that when the Government controls "gates to opportunity," it may not exclude qualified individuals based on "fixed notions concerning the roles and abilities of males and females."[81]

A similar case was brought before the Court in 2001. In this case an American serviceman brought his son home from Vietnam and raised him in America. He never did the paper work though to make his son a citizen. When the son got in trouble with the law after his eighteenth birthday, the fact that he was not an American citizen came to light and the government planned to deport him. The Court, once again, by majority opinion upheld the citizenship law that was in place. Fathers would continue to be denied automatic transmittal of citizenship to their children born abroad of foreign women.

## The House That Ruth (Ginsburg, not Babe) Built

The majority opinion, "stereotyping women as natural parents, strikes at the core of the house Ginsburg had built. . . . Many—even most—people behave in the ways their history and culture hands down. Ginsburg's project from the beginning was to remove that formal legal support for the old behaviors as a means to make room for new ways of acting."[82]

> One of Ginsburg's primary strategies was slowly to embed formal equality for women deeply in establishment thinking, using the law to categorize stereotyped treatment of women an "idea whose time has gone." . . . Her core strategy of protection for women's equality. Since 1971 she had been steadily advancing the case for women by building a structure of precedent . . . to treat women as individuals, not members of a class reduced to the average behavior of the group. . . . Specifically, women could not be lumped together and presumed to be dependent while men were typecast as self-sufficient.[83]

## Sandra's Last Case

In Sandra's last sex discrimination case before she stepped down from the Supreme Court bench, *Jackson v. Birmingham Board of Education*, she was again the critical swing vote. As such, she made sure that gender equality prevailed in this instance.

> Federal law, called Title IX, had long prohibited sex discrimination in schools that got federal funds. When a longtime physical education teacher, Roderick Jackson, got assigned to a new school and discovered his girls' basketball team was getting the short end of the court, he complained. His evaluations suddenly went south, and he was eventually fired.[84]

The ruling in this case not only upheld the prohibition of sex discrimination in schools that received federal funds, it expanded the protection to include those who blew the whistle on sex discrimination. In her written opinion Sandra stated, "Retaliation is discrimination 'on the basis of sex' because it is an intentional response to the nature of the complaint: an allegation of sex discrimination."[85]

## Dissenter in Chief

Sandra submitted her letter of resignation to President George W. Bush in June 2005. In her letter she stated she would step down when her replacement was confirmed. In September 2005 Justice Rehnquist died, leaving President Bush with two Supreme Court vacancies to fill. Once these vacancies were filled, conservative justices were in the majority and Ruth became "the dissenter in chief."[86] Another justice stepped down in 2009 and President Barack Obama appointed a woman, Sonia Sotomayor, to take his place. Another woman, Elena Kagan, joined the Court in 2010. Conservatives, however, were still in the majority.

"With its new majority now in place, the Court was just returning to recent disputes and rolling back the feminist legal revolution."[87] By 2013, much of the legal ground Ruth and Sandra had fought so hard to establish regarding gender equality was disappearing. The Court:

- narrowed the interpretation of who was eligible for benefits under the Family and Medical Leave Act;

- protected the employer from liability in a sex discrimination case;

- raised the standards for proving retaliation for blowing the whistle on sex discrimination and ruled that "any other good reason for firing the complaining employee would exonerate the employer";[88] and

- declared "that the section of the Voting Rights Act of 1965 requiring states such as Alabama to check with the Justice Department when tinkering with their election laws—a process called 'preclearance'—was unconstitutional."[89]

"Changing the culture on subjects such as affirmative action, defendants' rights, and employment discrimination is an agonizingly long process. That process depends in turn on the election of a president and a Senate inclined to seek appointments of a different mind-set. Before that can happen, the minds of people likely to seek office and the voters who elect them must change."[90]

This brings us full circle to the need for heart change.

# CHAPTER ELEVEN

# MY JOURNEY

As stated in chapter seven, the church failed women by not taking the lead in setting women free as Christ intended. Rather, the church has allowed the world to take the lead and has followed its example. Well, the world, at least the United States, is now leading in a new direction regarding gender equality. My question to Christ followers now is: Are you willing to take a good, hard, honest look at the lens through which you view reality, and consider the possibility that maybe the values and beliefs you were taught growing up regarding the roles of the sexes is not actually what Christ taught?

I know that what I'm asking is difficult and can make one feel uncomfortable and anxious. Believe me, I know how hard it is to take a serious look at beliefs you were taught growing up and deciding for yourself whether or not you agree with those beliefs. I know this because I have experienced it.

I grew up in an Irish Catholic family, attended Catholic schools for twelve years, and went to Mass every Sunday and holy day. I learned that God was a very cold, distant, critical God who didn't care about how I felt or what I needed, and who had very high expectations of me, so high it was doubtful I would ever reach them. I also learned that he wouldn't love me or welcome me home unless I met his expectations. This led me to decide that he certainly was not someone I could trust or depend on. Rather, he was someone to be afraid of and stay away from. I, therefore, drifted away from church and away from God in my early adulthood. I didn't miss anything in my life because church to me was performing empty rituals that I didn't understand and reciting memorized responses and prayers that I also didn't understand.

When I became a parent I decided to go back to church. It was important to me that my children develop good morals and values and I figured that the best way to make this happen was to raise them in church, though I knew I did not want to raise them in the Catholic Church. I found a protestant church I liked and started attending regularly. At first I was going for the kids, though it wasn't long before I started going for myself. I started hearing things like Christ died for me and God wanted a personal relationship with me. Those were totally foreign concepts to me and very difficult to wrap my mind around. What really blew my mind though was when I learned in a Bible study that there was no such thing as Purgatory. That was just too much and that brought into question everything I had been taught growing up. I felt like the rug had been pulled out from under me. It was *very* unsettling.

I then went through a period of questioning, searching, and deciding what I believed and what I didn't believe. I eventually came to the conclusion that the God of my childhood is not the real God. I began to believe that God really does love me and care about how I feel and what I need, and that he will take care of me and provide for me. I spent months reading Matthew 6:25–33 (see appendix two) every day. I slowly began to believe that if God takes care of the birds and the flowers, he will take care of me. I began to understand that he wants to be involved in my life day by day, minute by minute (not just for an hour on Sunday morning). I also slowly began to believe that he loves me so much that he sent his only Son, Jesus, to suffer and die for me and that Jesus would have suffered and died if I was the only person on the planet. I finally understood and believed that he wants me to have a relationship with Jesus and to follow Jesus, not a bunch of man-made rules like whether or not I eat meat on Friday. I also finally understood that there was nothing I could do to earn salvation, that it was a gift freely offered that I could either choose to accept or not accept. I chose to accept it and started my walk with Jesus.

As I walked with Jesus I gradually came to the realization that I had been given the spiritual gift of leadership. It took me a while to believe that I had been given this spiritual gift. It took me a while longer to embrace this belief. It took longer still before I understood how God wanted me to use that gift, and that's when the fun began. My church was getting ready to launch a Celebrate Recovery ministry and God let me know beyond the shadow of a doubt that he wanted me to lead the ministry. I stepped into the role of Celebrate Recovery Ministry Leader and began one of the most difficult years of my life.

One would think that once I knew what my spiritual gifts were and understood how God wanted me to use them, it would be clear sailing. Wrong! Nothing could be further from the truth. As I tried to live out the purpose God had called me to, using the gifts he gave me, I encountered intense opposition. My leadership was constantly challenged and undermined. I was told that I was controlling (a bad thing) and that I was too strong of a leader (another bad thing).

I studied the difference between controlling and leading. I studied the difference between leading and managing. I studied the difference between anointing and ordination. I read books on gender equality in the church, and I studied the lives of women in the Bible. (The women I studied are discussed in chapters four and six.)

I gradually came to understand that the pastors and leaders in the church wanted me to *manage* the ministry. They did *not* want me to lead it. In spite of this, I continued to operate in my gifts and do what God had called me to do. I *led* the ministry, and I eventually crashed right into the stained glass ceiling. I was removed from leadership of the Celebrate Recovery ministry by the pastors and some other leaders in the church.

Though this was an extremely painful time for me, I learned some important life lessons. One of the most important lessons I learned was, as we grow into the people God created us to be, we become more comfortable in our own skin. When we are comfortable in our own skin, we are able to unreservedly allow the people around us to be comfortable in their skin, to be who they are, who God created them to be. When we are not comfortable in our own skin, we often try to control our external circumstances and the people in our life in an effort to achieve that comfort. In her book *Men and Women in the Church*, Sarah Sumner, a noted author, international speaker, and dean at A. W. Tozer Theological Seminary, describes a time when she was impacted by people around her who were not comfortable in their own skins. "When I was a student at Trinity, one of my professors called me into his office and said to me in a warm, fatherly tone, 'Sarah, do not show the full color of your plume; it will intimidate the men.'" She further stated, "Every Christian woman is told not to lead too much."[91]

As I look back at the times I was told I was too strong of a leader and think about the people who told me this, I now understand that they were not comfortable in their own skins. If they were, they would not have been so threatened by me growing into the person and the leader God had anointed me to be.

As a result of all this I came to the unshakable conclusion that God is color-blind and gender-blind. He does not distribute gifts and assign purposes based on race or gender.

## New Passion

When I was a senior in high school I took a psychology course. I was fascinated by the concept that there are reasons why people do what they do and feel what they feel. This course was the beginning of a lifelong desire to understand what makes people tick. I subsequently majored in psychology in college, went to graduate school where I earned a master's degree in clinical social work, and embarked on a career as a psychotherapist. I also engaged in therapy myself as a client to understand what made me tick.

The desire to understand what makes people tick grew into a passion for helping people live healthy, happy lives emotionally and relationally. When God called me to lead a Celebrate Recovery ministry in August 2003, I was given another avenue through which to help people heal the hurts, habits, and hang-ups which impeded them from living the lives they were created to live.

In July 2014 God narrowed this passion to focus on women. He lit a fire in my heart to help his daughters be set free from the belief systems and practices that reinforce the inequality of the sexes and which stop women from being who God created them to be. Writing this book is one way I am putting form to this passion and living my new calling from God. I don't know what else he may want me to do to fulfill this calling. I don't need to know right now. I just need to keep putting one foot in front of the other, trusting that he will let me know what he wants me to do.

## Conflict: Good or Bad?

If God's daughters are to truly be set free to be who God created them to be, they need to be seen as equal to men in the eyes of the church. Just as Sandra Day O'Connor and Ruth Bader Ginsburg made women equal to men in the eyes of the law, people need to step forward who will work toward making women equal to men in the eyes of the church. Needless to say, this will be a long uphill battle which will cause much conflict and controversy.

Throughout my sixty years on the planet, I have met very few people who have a healthy attitude toward conflict. Rather, I have come across individuals who are either conflict creators or conflict avoiders. Conflict creators thrive on conflict and crave it. They therefore go out of their way to create it. Conflict avoiders, on the other hand, are uncomfortable with conflict and run from it as if running for their life.

As a former approval seeker and people pleaser *par excellence*, I fell into the category of conflict avoider. I gradually came to see though, that conflict is not inherently good or bad. It can be either productive or destructive depending on how it's handled. It also seems to be an inevitable and unavoidable ingredient for change, particularly social and/or political change. It's too bad it has to be this way, as I'm sure civil rights workers and women suffragists would attest to. However, it is what it is.

In church circles, I have met many people who believe that conflict and controversy in the church is not okay, and that it is not okay to question or challenge church leaders. If you believe this, I encourage you to read the four gospels and the book of Acts. They are full of accounts of Jesus and his apostles and disciples confronting and challenging the religious leaders of their time.

When Jesus began his earthly ministry he started a revolution. He, and later his apostles and disciples, worked to transition the religious people of his day from the old covenant (a covenant of works, a religious covenant which focused on behavior) to the new covenant (a covenant of faith, a relationship covenant which focuses on the heart).

Though many people easily made the transition, many others, primarily the religious leaders did not.

As Jesus continued his ministry many people believed in him and thronged to him. Mark 1:45 tells us, "Large crowds soon surrounded Jesus, and he couldn't publicly enter a town anywhere. He had to stay out in the secluded places, but people from everywhere kept coming to him." Matthew 4:24–25 tells us, "News about him spread as far as Syria, and people soon began bringing to him all who were sick. And whatever their sickness or disease, or if they were demon possessed or epileptic or paralyzed—he healed them all. Large crowds followed him wherever he went."

These people knew who Jesus was and where his power came from. Luke 9:42–43 recounts, "As the boy came forward, the demon knocked him to the ground and threw him into a violent convulsion. But Jesus rebuked the evil spirit and healed the boy. Then he gave him back to his father. Awe gripped the people as they saw this majestic display of God's power."

Others, primarily the religious leaders, refused to believe in Jesus. Though they witnessed his miracles, they closed their minds and hearts to the evidence their own eyes and ears were giving them. The greatest difficulty the religious leaders had with Jesus's teaching was that it ran counter to their belief in fanatical obedience to their laws. Throughout his earthly ministry, Jesus taught that grace, compassion, and love are more important than the law. The religious leaders refused to change their thinking. They held on to their belief that obedience to their rules and laws was more important than showing love and compassion to those who were hurting.

There are religious leaders today who are holding on just as tightly to their beliefs regarding the inequality of the sexes and roles which are appropriate for women vs. roles which are appropriate for men. I have encountered a few of them. Though they have not beaten me, whipped me, imprisoned me, or had me killed (which the religious leaders of Jesus's day did to him and many of his apostles and disciples), they have refused to allow me to serve in their congregations. They have not been able to stop me from following Jesus, though, and doing what he called me to do. They were not successful in this because I have learned how to live my life for an audience of One. I do this because it fills me with an internal peace and joy that the world cannot give. This peace and joy can only come from God. I also do it because when I stand before God one day, I want to hear him say, "Well done, good and faithful servant."

I also want my sisters in Christ to hear this when they stand before God. I want them to be who they were created to be, to be free to operate in their spiritual gifts, and to fulfill the purpose for which they were created and designed to fulfill. I want the church to not only give them permission to pursue their calling, but to also actively encourage and support them in doing so. I want the church to tell them they are on equal footing with men and don't need to fit themselves into prescribed roles.

Needless to say, we have a long way to go to make this happen. There are a lot of battles which will need to be fought and many bodies of water in which individuals will need to swim upstream. Much conflict and controversy will follow. Whoever chooses to fight these battles or swim up these streams will need to be ready and willing to face a torrent of opposition. It will take people who have the determination of James Madison, the visionary leadership of Elizabeth Stanton, the dedication of Susan B. Anthony, the perseverance of Martin Luther King Jr., the amazing selflessness of the Freedom Riders, and the passion of Ruth Bader Ginsburg. Most of all though, it will take people whose hearts have been changed by Christ.

# CHAPTER TWELVE

# PETER: A PORTRAIT OF A CHANGED HEART

Peter was among the first disciples of Jesus Christ, if not *the* first disciple. Prior to meeting Jesus, Peter was a fisherman. He was also a family man.

Peter was born in Bethsaida, a small fishing village on the banks of the Jordan River, not far from the Sea of Galilee. His family was Jewish and practiced strict obedience to the Jewish law. Peter's education probably ended when he was about thirteen, at which time he probably started working as a fisherman.

When Peter met Jesus, he was living in Capernaum, on the shores of the Sea of Galilee, and fishing with his brother Andrew. They worked in close partnership with a man named Zebedee and Zebedee's sons, James and John.

Fishing in the first century was extremely demanding physically, quite unlike fishing in the twenty-first century. First-century fishermen were tough, strong, unkempt, shabbily dressed, and often used vulgar language. They must also have been somewhat fearless because unbelievably strong storms tended to come up on the Sea of Galilee quickly and unexpectedly. These storms could easily capsize the twenty- to thirty-foot boats the fisherman used.

There are varying accounts as to how Peter became a disciple of Jesus Christ. Mark's and Matthew's accounts are virtually identical. "One day as Jesus was walking along the shore of the Sea of Galilee, he saw two brothers—Simon, also called Peter, and Andrew—throwing a net into the water, for they fished for a living. Jesus called out to them, 'Come, follow me, and I will show you how to fish for people!' And they left their nets at once and followed him" (Matthew 4:18–20). Luke recounts the same incident, however, he expands the story including much more detail.

> One day as Jesus was preaching on the shore of the Sea of Galilee, great crowds pressed in on him to listen to the word of God. He noticed two empty boats at the water's edge, for the fishermen had left them and were washing their nets. Stepping into one of the boats, Jesus asked Simon, its owner, to push it out into the water. So he sat in the boat and taught the crowds from there.
>
> When he had finished speaking, he said to Simon, "Now go out where it is deeper, and let down your nets to catch some fish."
>
> "Master," Simon replied, "we worked hard all last night and didn't catch a thing. But if you

say so, I'll let the nets down again." And this time their nets were so full of fish they began to tear! A shout for help brought their partners in the other boat, and soon both boats were filled with fish and on the verge of sinking.

When Simon Peter realized what had happened, he fell to his knees before Jesus and said, "Oh Lord, please leave me—I'm such a sinful man." For he was awestruck by the number of fish they had caught, as were the others with him. His partners, James and John, the sons of Zebedee, were also amazed.

Jesus replied to Simon, "Don't be afraid! From now on you'll be fishing for people!" And as soon as they landed, they left everything and followed Jesus." (Luke 5:1–11)

Mark's and Matthew's tellings of the story are a bit hard for me to swallow. I would not drop everything and follow a complete stranger simply because he or she told me to. I don't know many people who would do that. Luke's version of the story, however, makes it more believable. I imagine Peter must have been impressed or touched by Jesus's teaching, which was why he called him "Master" and took his boat out again on Jesus's "say so." When their nets became filled to overflowing with fish, Peter "realized what had happened" and reacted with humility. Peter seems to have instantly known that Jesus was someone special and extraordinary. He also seems to have known that he didn't deserve to be around someone so special and extraordinary.

We know that Peter had a family because in the gospel of Matthew, chapter 8, Peter's mother-in-law is referenced, and in a letter Peter himself wrote to one of the early churches, he references a son. "Your sister church here in Babylon sends you greetings, and so does my son Mark" (1 Peter 5:13). When Jesus called him to be a disciple, Peter walked away from his family and his job to follow Jesus, most probably not having the faintest clue what his future would hold.

However it happened that Jesus called Peter to follow him, Jesus undoubtedly called Peter to be his follower and Peter responded. Even though Peter turned his whole life upside down to follow Jesus, I believe it is highly unlikely that Peter grasped who Jesus truly was when he first became his disciple. I believe it is much more likely that this understanding developed as he watched and listened to Jesus over a period of time.

## Watching and Listening

Immediately after Peter began to follow him, "Jesus traveled throughout the region of Galilee, teaching in the synagogues and announcing the Good News about the Kingdom. And he healed every kind of disease and illness. News about him spread as far as Syria, and people soon began bringing to him all who were sick. And whatever their sickness or disease, or if they were demon possessed or epileptic or paralyzed—he healed them all" (Matthew 4:23–24).

The four gospels are full of accounts of Jesus teaching and healing. We don't know for sure that Peter was with Jesus when all these events occurred, however, we can be fairly certain that he was present for most, if not all, of these occurrences. A fraction of the recorded, miraculous things Jesus did during his three-year earthly ministry are as follows:

- Changed water into wine at the wedding feast in Cana (John 2:1–11)

- Healed a man with leprosy (Matthew 8:1–4; Mark 1:40–45; Luke 5:12–16)

- Healed a paralyzed man (Matthew 9:1–8; Mark 2:1–12; Luke 5:17–26)

- Healed a lame man (John 5:1–15)

- Healed demon possessed men (Matthew 12:22–23; Mark 1:21–26)

- Raised a widow's son from the dead (Luke 7:11–17)

We can assume that Peter was indeed present at the event involving his mother-in-law and witnessed the following happenings: "When Jesus arrived at Peter's house, Peter's mother-in-law was sick in bed with a high fever. But when Jesus touched her hand, the fever left her. Then she got up and prepared a meal for him. That evening many demon-possessed people were brought to Jesus. He cast out the evil spirits with a simple command, and he healed all the sick" (Matthew 8:14–16).

After hearing and seeing all that Jesus said and did during this time, Peter must have, at the very least, been entertaining the notion that Jesus was indeed the Son of God, the long-awaited Messiah, as he claimed to be. (See appendix three.)

I would now like to describe a series of events that, due to the way they are recorded in the four gospels, seemingly occurred consecutively over a period of a day or two.

> As evening came, Jesus said to his disciples, "Let's cross to the other side of the lake." So they took Jesus in the boat and started out, leaving the crowds behind (although other boats followed). But soon a fierce storm came up. High waves were breaking into the boat, and it began to fill with water.
>
> Jesus was sleeping at the back of the boat with his head on a cushion. The disciples woke him up, shouting, "Teacher, don't you care that we're going to drown?"
>
> When Jesus woke up, he rebuked the wind and said to the waves, "Silence! Be still!" Suddenly the wind stopped, and there was a great calm. Then he asked them, "Why are you afraid? Do you still have no faith?"
>
> The disciples were absolutely terrified. "Who is this man?" they asked each other. "Even the wind and waves obey him!" (Mark 4:35–41)

Immediately after calming the storm Jesus healed a demon possessed man.

So they arrived at the other side of the lake, in the region of the Gerasenes. When Jesus climbed out of the boat, a man possessed by an evil spirit came out from the tombs to meet him. This man lived in the burial caves and could no longer be restrained, even with a chain. Whenever he was put into chains and shackles—as he often was—he snapped the chains from his wrists and smashed the shackles. No one was strong enough to subdue him. Day and night he wandered among the burial caves and in the hills, howling and cutting himself with sharp stones.

When Jesus was still some distance away, the man saw him, ran to meet him, and bowed low before him. With a shriek, he screamed, "Why are you interfering with me, Jesus, Son of the Most High God? In the name of God, I beg you, don't torture me!" For Jesus had already said to the spirit, "Come out of the man, you evil spirit."

Then Jesus demanded, "What is your name?"

And he replied, "My name is Legion, because there are many of us inside this man." Then the evil spirits begged him again and again not to send them to some distant place.

There happened to be a large herd of pigs feeding on the hillside nearby. "Send us into those pigs," the spirits begged. "Let us enter them."

So Jesus gave them permission. The evil spirits came out of the man and entered the pigs, and the entire herd of about 2,000 pigs plunged down the steep hillside into the lake and drowned in the water.

The herdsman fled to the nearby town and the surrounding countryside, spreading the news as they ran. People rushed out to see what had happened. A crowd soon gathered around Jesus, and they saw the man who had been possessed by the legion of demons. He was sitting there fully clothed and perfectly sane, and they were all afraid. (Mark 5:1–15)

Then, after healing the demon possessed man, Jesus healed a woman with an issue of bleeding and raised a young girl from the dead.

Jesus got into the boat again and went back to the other side of the lake, where a large crowd gathered around him on the shore. Then a leader of the local synagogue, whose name was Jairus, arrived. When he saw Jesus, he fell at his feet, pleading fervently with him. "My little daughter is dying," he said. "Please come and lay your hands on her; heal her so she can live."

Jesus went with him, and all the people followed, crowding around him. A woman in the crowd had suffered for twelve years with constant bleeding. She had suffered a great deal from many doctors, and over the years she had spent everything she had to pay them, but she had gotten no better. In fact, she had gotten worse. She had heard about Jesus, so she came up behind him through the crowd and touched his robe. For she thought to herself, "If I can just touch his robe, I will be healed." Immediately the bleeding stopped, and she could feel in her body that she had been healed of her terrible condition.

Jesus realized at once that healing power had gone out from him, so he turned around in the crowd and asked, "Who touched my robe?"

His disciples said to him, "Look at this crowd pressing around you. How can you ask 'Who touched me?'"

But he kept on looking around to see who had done it. Then the frightened woman, trembling at the realization of what had happened to her, came and fell to her knees in front of him and told him what she had done. And he said to her, "Daughter, your faith has made you well. Go in peace. Your suffering is over."

While he was speaking to her, messengers arrived from the home of Jairus, the leader of the synagogue. They told him, "Your daughter is dead. There's no use troubling the Teacher now."

But Jesus overheard them and said to Jairus, "Don't be afraid. Just have faith."

Then Jesus stopped the crowd and wouldn't let anyone go on with him except Peter, James, and John (the brother of James). When they came to the home of the synagogue leader, Jesus saw much commotion and weeping and wailing. He went inside and asked, "Why all this commotion and weeping? The child isn't dead; she's only asleep."

The crowd laughed at him. But he made them all leave, and he took the girl's father and mother and his three disciples into the room where the girl was lying. Holding her hand, he said to her, "*Talitha koum*," which means "Little girl, get up!" And the girl, who was twelve years old, immediately stood up and walked around! They were overwhelmed and totally amazed. (Mark 5:21–42)

After Jesus left [Jairus's] home, two blind men followed along behind him, shouting, "Son of David, have mercy on us!"

They went right into the house where he was staying, and Jesus asked them, "Do you believe I can make you see?"

"Yes, Lord," they told him, "we do."

Then he touched their eyes and said, "Because of your faith, it will happen." Then their eyes were opened, and they could see! (Matthew 9:27–30).

Jesus still wasn't done for the day. After this "a demon-possessed man who couldn't speak was brought to Jesus. So Jesus cast out the demon, and then the man began to speak" (Matthew 9:32–33).

Peter must have been on sensory overload by this time, totally overwhelmed by what he had seen and heard. We are not sure if, by the end of this day, Peter truly believed that Jesus was the Son of God, the long-awaited Messiah. It is hard to imagine though that he wouldn't have believed by this time. At some point, Peter did obviously embrace the truth that Jesus truly was the Son of God, the long-awaited Messiah, because he stepped out of his comfort zone in a huge way.

## Embracing the Truth

Immediately after this, Jesus insisted that his disciples get back into the boat and cross to the other side of the lake, while he sent the people home. After sending them home, he went up into the hills by himself to pray. Night fell while he was there alone.

Meanwhile, the disciples were in trouble far away from land, for a strong wind had risen, and they were fighting heavy waves. About three o'clock in the morning Jesus came toward them, walking on the water. When the disciples saw him walking on the water, they were terrified. In their fear, they cried out, "It's a ghost!"

But Jesus spoke to them at once. "Don't be afraid," he said. "Take courage. I am here!"

Then Peter called to him, "Lord, if it's really you, tell me to come to you, walking on the water."

"Yes, come," Jesus said.

So Peter went over the side of the boat and walked on the water toward Jesus. But when he saw the strong wind and the waves, he was terrified and began to sink. "Save me, Lord!" he shouted.

Jesus immediately reached out and grabbed him. "You have so little faith," Jesus said. "Why did you doubt me?"

When they climbed back into the boat, the wind stopped. Then the disciples worshipped him. "You really are the Son of God!" they exclaimed. (Matthew 14:22–33)

After this, Peter's belief that Jesus was the Son of God seems to have become deeply rooted in him. He became bolder. He evidenced this boldness and certainty in the following incidents: "Many of his disciples turned away and deserted him. Then Jesus turned to the Twelve and asked, 'Are you also going to leave?' Simon Peter replied, 'Lord, to whom would we go? You have the words that give eternal life. We believe, and we know you are the Holy One of God'" (John 6:66–69).

"Jesus and his disciples left Galilee and went up to the villages near Caesarea Philippi. As they were walking along, he asked them, "Who do people say I am?"

"Well," they replied, "some say John the Baptist, some say Elijah, and others say you are one of the other prophets."

Then he asked them, "But who do you say I am?"

Peter replied, "You are the Messiah." (Mark 8:27–29)

Jesus rewarded Peter's boldness and statements of certainty by allowing him to experience the following:

Jesus took Peter and the two brothers, James and John, and led them up a high mountain to be alone. As the men watched, Jesus' appearance was transformed so that his face shone like the sun, and his clothes became as white as light. Suddenly, Moses and Elijah appeared and began talking with Jesus.

Peter exclaimed, "Lord, it's wonderful to be here! If you want, I'll make three shelters as memorials—one for you, one for Moses, and one for Elijah."

But even as he spoke, a bright cloud overshadowed them, and a voice from the cloud said, "This is my dearly loved Son, who brings me great joy. Listen to him." The disciples were terrified and fell face down on the ground.

Then Jesus came over and touched them. "Get up," he said. "Don't be afraid." And when they looked up, Moses and Elijah were gone, and they saw only Jesus. (Matthew 17:1–8)

I imagine this must have completely cemented Peter's belief that Jesus really was the Son of God, the long-awaited Messiah. I'm also guessing that Jesus must have known Peter would need the memory of this experience to carry him through the days, weeks, months, and years that were ahead of him.

> "During the forty days after he suffered and died, he appeared to the apostles from time to time, and he proved to them in many ways that he was actually alive. And he talked to them about the Kingdom of God.
>
> Once when he was eating with them, he commanded them, 'Do not leave Jerusalem until the Father sends you the gift he promised, as I told you before. John baptized with water, but in just a few days you will be baptized with the Holy Spirit. . . . You will receive power when the Holy Spirit comes upon you. And you will be my witnesses, telling people about me everywhere—in Jerusalem, throughout Judea, in Samaria, and to the ends of the earth.'" (Acts 1:3–5, 8)

During one of the times that Jesus appeared to the apostles after his death and resurrection from the dead, he challenged Peter. I believe Jesus was testing Peter's commitment to follow him.

After breakfast Jesus asked Simon Peter, "Simon son of John, do you love me more than these?"

"Yes, Lord," Peter replied, "you know I love you."

"Then feed my lambs," Jesus told him.

Jesus repeated the question: "Simon son of John, do you love me?"

"Yes, Lord," Peter said, "you know I love you."

"Then take care of my sheep," Jesus said.

A third time he asked him, "Simon son of John, do you love me?"

Peter was hurt that Jesus asked the question a third time. He said, "Lord, you know everything. You know that I love you."

Jesus said, "Then feed my sheep." (John 21:15–17)

Jesus then went on to tell Peter, "I tell you the truth, when you were young, you were able to do as you liked; you dressed yourself and went wherever you wanted to go. But when you are old, you will stretch out your hands, and others will dress you and take you where you don't want to go" (John 21:18).

"The expression 'to stretch out your hands,' means absolutely nothing to us today, but to a person of Peter's time it was a clear reference to crucifixion."[92]

I believe it is a distinct possibility that Jesus asked Peter the same question (Do you love me?) three times and gave him the same command (in essence, Take care of my followers) three times because Jesus needed to drive home to Peter that it would be Peter's love for Jesus that would be the driving force, the motivator that would carry Peter to complete the work Jesus had assigned to him, and Peter did complete his work.

As Jesus promised, the Holy Spirit came to the disciples on Pentecost. Once they were empowered by the Holy Spirit, Peter and the other apostles and disciples began to carry on Jesus's work in Jerusalem. Peter healed a crippled beggar (Acts 3:1–8); he preached in the temple (Acts 3:12–26); and he was questioned and threatened by Jewish leaders (Acts 4:5–22).

Peter, along with the other apostles and disciples though, continued to minister in Jesus's name. They did not let opposition, including eventual arrest, stop them.

> The apostles were performing many miraculous signs and wonders among the people. . . . More and more people believed and were brought to the Lord—crowds of both men and women. As a result of the apostles' work, sick people were brought out into the streets on beds and mats so that Peter's shadow might fall across some of them as he went by. Crowds came from the villages around Jerusalem, bringing their sick and those possessed by evil spirits, and they were all healed." (Acts 5:12, 14–16)

Peter and the other apostles continued to be harassed and arrested by religious leaders who repeatedly ordered them not to teach about Jesus. The apostles, however, did not let human beings stop them from doing the work they had been commissioned and anointed to do. "Peter and the apostles replied, 'We must obey God rather than any human authority'" (Acts 5:29). The religious leaders then stepped up their opposition against the apostles. It did not, however, deter the apostles one bit. They continued to teach and to heal in Jesus's name. "So God's message continued to spread. The number of believers greatly increased in Jerusalem, and many of the Jewish priests were converted, too" (Acts 6:7).

Peter was eventually arrested and imprisoned. The prison guards were not able to keep him in prison though. God sent an angel to set him free (Acts 12:3–11). Following this incident,

> Peter seemed never to have returned to Jerusalem to stay. . . . Peter spent many years traveling throughout the Near East. He visited the Christian communities which were springing up all over that area, preaching, teaching, and making sure that the new converts fell into no heresy. . . . Peter also resided for a time in Antioch. A large city of about a million people, it was located in what is now the nation of Syria, about seventeen miles east of the Mediterranean coast. . . .
>
> Peter eventually went to Rome and lived there during his latter years. . . . There were between thirty and forty thousand Jews living in Rome in the first century. . . . Peter's popularity increased rapidly with many converts made in Rome. . . .

On the night of July 19, A.D. 64, fire broke out in a wooden shed at the foot of the Caelian and Palatine hills in Rome, and spread to the small shops nearby. Within hours, much of the city was engulfed by flames which burned out of control for nine days, destroying two thirds of Rome and killing hundreds. Nero blamed the Christians for the disaster. Had not Peter and Paul publicly proclaimed that the world would end in fire? Therefore, they must have been responsible. He denounced Christianity as a "deadly superstition," and accused Christians of being haters of the human race and perpetrators of such crimes as drinking the blood of babies in Holy Communion. Thus he marked the Church for extermination.[93]

Eventually, on a date no one is exactly sure of, Peter was crucified. According to William Steuart McBirnie, in his book *The Search for the Twelve Apostles*, Peter spent nine months in a Roman prison prior to his death.

Maliciously condemned, Peter was cast into the horrible, fetid prison of the Mamertine. There, for nine months, in absolute darkness, he endured monstrous torture manacled to a post. . . .

This dreaded place is known by two names. In classical history it is referred to as

Gemonium or the Tullian Keep. In later secular history it is best known as the Mamertine....

The Mamertine is described as a deep cell cut out of solid rock at the foot of the capitol, consisting of two chambers, one over the other. The only entrance is through an aperture in the ceiling. The lower chamber was the death cell. Light never entered and it was never cleaned. The awful stench and filth generated a poison fatal to the inmates of the dungeon, the most awful ever known....

How Peter managed to survive those nine long dreadful months is beyond human imagination. During his entire incarceration he was manacled in an upright position, chained to the column, unable to lay down to rest.... History tells us the amazing fact that in spite of all the suffering Peter was subjected to, he converted his gaolers, Processus, Martinianus, and forty-seven others.[94]

I would hypothesize that Peter managed to survive his imprisonment and convert his jailers because he was a tough, strong, fearless fisherman whose heart had been changed by Christ and who was empowered by the Holy Spirit to weather fierce storms.

# CHAPTER THIRTEEN

# CONUNDRUM

Before I end this book I would like to discuss the conundrum of success. In case you're not sure what a conundrum is, it is:

- Anything that puzzles (dictionary.com)

- A question or problem having only a conjectural answer; an intricate and difficult problem (Merriam-Webster's Dictionary)

- A confusing and difficult problem or question (Merriam-Webster's Dictionary)

Success, in my opinion, is a conundrum because it means different things to different people. It is also difficult to measure. After all, how do you know when enough success is enough? Some dictionary definitions of success are:

- The favorable or prosperous termination of attempts or endeavors; the accomplishment of one's goals; the attainment of wealth, position, honors, or the like (dictionary.com)

- The fact of getting or achieving wealth, respect, or fame; the correct or desired result of an attempt (Merriam-Webster's Dictionary)

- The accomplishment of an aim or purpose; the attainment of fame, wealth, or social status (Merriam-Webster's Dictionary)

As stated above, success means different things to different people. Here are a few individuals' definitions of success:

- Success is the ability to go from failure to failure without losing your enthusiasm. —Winston Churchill

- Success is a matter of adjusting one's efforts to obstacles and one's abilities to a service needed by others.—Henry Ford

- Success is doing ordinary things extra-ordinarily well.—Jim Rohn

- Success in life could be defined as the continued expansion of happiness and the progressive realization of worthy goals. —Deepak Chopra

- Success is . . . knowing God and his desires for me; growing to my maximum potential; and sowing seeds that benefit others. —John Maxwell

As for myself, my definition of success is to faithfully walk the path carved out for me by God, fulfilling the purposes he assigned to me and designed me to fulfill. "Let us run with endurance the race God has set before us" (Hebrews 12:1); and to be able to say with confidence at the end of my life, "I have fought the good fight, I have finished the race; and I have remained faithful" (2 Timothy 4:7). My ultimate measure of success will be to hear, when I stand before God, "Well done, good and faithful servant."

I believe that it behooves every adult to develop an individual definition of success. I further believe that it is particularly important for those of us who are Christ followers to develop an individual definition of success. The reason for this is that Christ followers need to settle the question of whether they will define success according to the world's standards or according to God's standards.

Jesus addressed the issue of defining and measuring success in the Sermon on the Mount. "Don't store up treasures here on earth, where moths eat them and rust destroys them, and where thieves break in and steal. Store your treasures in heaven, where moths and rust cannot destroy, and thieves do not break in and steal. Wherever your treasure is, there the desires of your heart will also be. ... No one can serve two masters. For you will hate one and love the other; you will be devoted to one and despise the other. You cannot serve both God and money" (Matthew 6:19–21, 24). Therefore, I believe the central question each Christ follower needs to answer for himself or herself, is "Why am I doing what I do?"

God is a God of hearts. He is not nearly as interested in what we do as in why we do it. He is not pleased by right behavior if it is fueled by wrong motives. Right behavior flows from a right heart, not vice versa. Matthew 12:35 says, "A good person produces good things from the treasury of a good heart, and an evil person produces evil things from the treasury of an evil heart." Therefore, those of us who are committed to protesting gender inequality in the church need to make sure we are operating out of pure motives. We need to always keep in mind the critical difference between effecting change in the world and effecting change in the church that was discussed in the introduction. In other words, fighting for gender equality in the church is not about women's rights or affirmative action. It is about spiritual liberation. It is not about women leading the church. It is about truly allowing Christ to be the head of the church by following the leading of the Holy Spirit when choosing who will serve in what ministry roles. It is about allowing individuals with the spiritual gift of leadership to lead and allowing individuals with the spiritual gift of preaching, to preach, *regardless of their gender.*

As we swim upstream to advocate or fight for gender equality in the church, conflict and controversy will inevitably follow. We need to face it head on and deal with it in healthy ways. That's what Jesus and the early apostles did when conflict and controversy erupted in response to their efforts to transition people from the old covenant to the new covenant. However, we cannot be conflict creators. We cannot create conflict for the sake of creating conflict.

If we do that we are not operating out of pure motives. On the other hand, we cannot be conflict avoiders. If we are conflict avoiders we are operating out of fear, and "God has not given us a spirit of fear and timidity, but of power, love, and self-discipline" (2 Timothy 1:7).

*Very important note:* Those of us who are called to fight for gender equality in the church need to be careful about how we measure success. We need to remember that we can only control what we do, we cannot control what anyone else does in response to what we do. We also need to remember that this change in the church will only come when hearts change, and we cannot change hearts. Only God can change a heart. He may use us as instruments to change hearts, but he is the one who does the heart changing.

Finally, I would like to leave you with the story of how and when Peter changed his definition of success. It happened during one of the times Jesus appeared to his apostles after his crucifixion.

> Later, Jesus appeared again to the disciples beside the Sea of Galilee. This is how it happened. Several of the disciples were there—Simon Peter, Thomas (nicknamed the Twin), Nathanael from Cana in Galilee, the sons of Zebedee, and two other disciples.
>
> Simon Peter said, "I'm going fishing."
>
> "We'll come too," they all said. So they went out in the boat, but they caught nothing all night.

At dawn Jesus was standing on the beach, but the disciples couldn't see who he was. He called out, "Fellows, have you caught any fish?"

"No," they replied.

Then he said, "Throw out your net on the right-hand side of the boat, and you'll get some!" So they did, and they couldn't haul in the net because there were so many fish in it.

Then the disciple Jesus loved said to Peter, "It's the Lord!" When Simon Peter heard that it was the Lord, he put on his tunic (for he had stripped for work), jumped into the water, and headed to shore. The others stayed with the boat and pulled the loaded net to the shore, for they were only about a hundred yards from shore. When they got there, they found breakfast waiting for them—fish cooking over a charcoal fire, and some bread.

"Bring some of the fish you've just caught," Jesus said. So Simon Peter went aboard and dragged the net to the shore. There were 153 large fish, and yet the net hadn't torn.

"Now come and have some breakfast!" Jesus said. None of the disciples dared to ask him, "Who are you?" They knew it was the Lord. Then Jesus served them the bread and the fish. This was the third time Jesus had appeared to his disciples since he had been raised from the dead." (John 21:1–14)

Bruce Wilkinson, in his book *Secrets of the Vine,* discussed the above incident. He wrote:

> Apparently without hesitation, the men in their battered boats pull in their nets and fling them over the other side. Soon they haul up such a net-straining catch of fish that they know beyond doubt who that man in the mist is. "It is the Lord," John says to Peter. And you know what Peter does next. In your mind's eye you can see Peter look toward shore. You can see him drop his hold on the net, plant his foot on the bow of the boat, and take that beautiful, flying leap into the waters of grace. . . . When Peter jumped, he forever left behind his little dreams of success. He left behind his doubts about God's plans for him and his stubborn insistence that things should turn out according to his expectations. He left behind any thought that his sins outweighed God's forgiveness. That impulsive leap marked the moment of Peter's breakthrough to a life of remarkable abundance. . . . God used him to be the new church's first leader, to preach to thousands, and to bring healing and the Holy Spirit.[95]

In that moment Peter changed his definition of success.

# AFTERWORD

A number of years ago I read an article in a Psychology Today magazine titled *Whistleblowing* (by Myron Peretz Glazer and Penina Migdal Glazer, August 1986 issue). This article resonated with me (which is why I held onto it). It seems that when I was young I was endowed with an absolute inability to tolerate injustice, oppression, dishonesty and a variety of "isms." To complement this, I was not endowed with an ability to keep my mouth shut. Due to this combination of characteristics, I have been a whistleblower my entire life and, believe me, this has not won me a whole lot of friends. What it is has given me though is a clear conscience and an ability to tolerate opposition.

The following excerpt, I believe, is a fairly accurate description of me:

> Virtually all of the ethical resisters we studied had long histories of successful employment. They were not alienated or politically active members of movements advocating major changes in society. On the contrary, they

began as firm believers in their organizations, convinced that if they took a grievance to superiors, there would be an appropriate response. This naivete led them into a series of damaging traps. They found that their earlier service and dedication provided them with little protection against charges of undermining organizational morale and effectiveness. Punishment took many forms— transfer, demotion, firing, blackballing, personal harassment, and intimidation. The first step was usually to undermine the effectiveness and reputation of whistleblowers by isolating them or assigning them to lesser duties or none at all.

The article also contained words of advice from more than twenty resisters. I found most of the advice to be solid and worthwhile. One word of advice that I did not agree with, though, was "Don't tilt at windmills; don't waste your strength and courage fighting a battle you know you will lose. There are more than enough fights around that offer a chance of winning." Rather than agreeing with and heeding this bit of advice, I agree with the statement made by Martin Sheen's character in the movie *An American President*, which I referenced in chapter three, "Don't fight the fights you can win, fight the fights that need fighting!"

In addition to getting this article out and reading and rereading it as encouragement as I wrote this book, I read the book *Sacred Pathways* by Gary Thomas. That book is about spiritual temperaments. Our spiritual temperament, or our sacred pathway, is "the way we relate to God, how we draw near to him."[96] By way of explanation, Thomas stated:

> Within the Christian faith there are many different and acceptable ways of demonstrating our love for God. Our temperaments will cause us to be more comfortable in some of these expressions than others—and that is perfectly acceptable to God. In fact, by worshipping God according to the way he made us, we are affirming his work as Creator.[97]

Of the nine sacred pathways Thomas identified, two of them describe how I draw near to God. Those two sacred pathways are sensate and activist.

In describing someone with a sensate spiritual temperament, Thomas says, "When these Christians worship, they want to be filled with sights, sounds, and smells that overwhelm them. . . . The five senses are God's most effective inroad to their hearts."[98]

In describing someone with an activist spiritual temperament or sacred pathway, Thomas says,

> They define worship as standing against evil and calling sinners to repentance. These Christians often view the church as a place to recharge their batteries so they can go back into the world to wage war against injustice. . . . They find their home in the rough-and-tumble world of confrontation. They are

energized more by interaction with others, even in conflict, than by being alone or in small groups.[99]

Other statements he made regarding the activist sacred pathway are as follows:

- "It can take some time for the enthusiasm generated by the activist mentality to be tempered and seasoned by maturity and foresight."[100]

- "Every activist must learn that faithful obedience doesn't always result in immediate success."[101]

- "Activists will never be satisfied playing it safe. They need to experience the exhilaration of seeing a miraculous God come through in miraculous ways."[102]

- "Activism is one temperament that, while it tends to spiritually feed many Christians, can also exhaust them."[103]

For many, many years I did not like my tendency to be a whistleblower. I wished I wasn't like that and I tried to change it. I tried to be oblivious or tolerant of injustice and oppression. It never worked. I tried valiantly to keep my mouth shut about injustices and wrongs I saw. I failed even more miserably at that. Then, when I read *Sacred Pathways* and realized God had wired me to be an activist, I finally relaxed about that part of myself and actually embraced it. I do wish, though, that my tempering and seasoning had happened a bit sooner. I might have made a few more friends if it had.

The more I studied it and thought about it, I realized that the activist temperament is my primary sacred pathway and the sensate temperament is my secondary pathway. I have felt that spiritual exhaustion when I am absolutely running on empty both emotionally and spiritually. When I am in a worship service where the music is excellent and the worship leader is worshipping, not entertaining, I can engage in authentic and meaningful individual worship. I then feel spiritually nurtured and energized and ready to take on the world. I realized that when God wired me to be an activist he knew about how exhausted and depleted I would get, so he wired me with the secondary pathway of sensate so I could be replenished and energized. Isn't he a wonderful God?!

Because God planted a passion inside me for a very specific calling and wired me with the temperament to fulfill this calling, I will not refuse to do the something I can do. I hope you do too.

# APPENDIX ONE

## The Sermon on the Mount

One day as he saw the crowds gathering, Jesus went up on the mountainside and sat down. His disciples gathered around him, and he began to teach them.

## The Beatitudes

"God blesses those who are poor and realize
their need for him,
for the Kingdom of Heaven is theirs.
God blesses those who mourn,
for they will be comforted.
God blesses those who are humble,
for they will inherit the whole earth.
God blesses those who hunger and thirst for
justice,
for they will be satisfied.
God blesses those who are merciful,
for they will be shown mercy.
God blesses those whose hearts are pure,
for they will see God.

God blesses those who work for peace,
    for they will be called the children of God.
God blesses those who are persecuted for doing
    right,
    for the Kingdom of Heaven is theirs.

"God blesses you when people mock you and persecute you and lie about you and say all sorts of evil things against you because you are my followers. Be happy about it! Be very glad! For a great reward awaits you in heaven. And remember, the ancient prophets were persecuted in the same way.

## Teaching about Salt and Light

"You are the salt of the earth. But what good is salt if it has lost its flavor? Can you make it salty again? It will be thrown out and trampled underfoot as worthless.

"You are the light of the world—like a city on a hilltop that cannot be hidden. No one lights a lamp and then puts it under a basket. Instead, a lamp is placed on a stand, where it gives light to everyone in the house. In the same way, let your good deeds shine out for all to see, so that everyone will praise your heavenly Father.

## Teaching about the Law

"Don't misunderstand why I have come. I did not come to abolish the law of Moses or the writings of the prophets. No, I came to accomplish their purpose. I tell you the truth, until heaven and earth disappear, not even the smallest detail of God's law will disappear until it until its purpose is achieved.

So if you ignore the least commandment and teach others to do the same, you will be called the least in the Kingdom of Heaven. But anyone who obeys God's laws and teaches them will be called great in the Kingdom of Heaven.

"But I warn you—unless your righteousness is better than the righteousness of the teachers of religious law and the Pharisees, you will never enter the Kingdom of Heaven!

## Teaching about Anger

"You have heard that our ancestors were told, 'You must not murder. If you commit murder, you are subject to judgment.' But I say, if you are even angry with someone, you are subject to judgment! If you call someone an idiot, you are in danger of being brought before the court. And if you curse someone, you are in danger of the fires of hell.

"So if you are presenting a sacrifice at the altar in the Temple and you suddenly remember that someone has something against you, leave your sacrifice there at the altar. Go and be reconciled to that person. Then come and offer your sacrifice to God.

"When you are on the way to court with your adversary, settle your differences quickly. Otherwise, your accuser may hand you over to the judge, who will hand you over to an officer, and you will be thrown into prison. And if that happens, you surely won't be free again until you have paid the last penny.

## Teaching about Adultery

"You have heard the commandment that says, 'You must not commit adultery.' But I say, anyone who even looks at a woman with lust has already committed adultery with her in his heart. So if your eye—even your good eye—causes you to lust, gouge it out and throw it away. It is better for you to lose one part of your body than for your whole body to be thrown into hell. And if your hand—even your stronger hand—causes you to sin, cut it off and throw it away. It is better for you to lose one part of your body than for your whole body to be thrown into hell.

## Teaching about Divorce

"You have heard the law that says, 'A man can divorce his wife by merely giving her a written notice of divorce.' But I say that a man who divorces his wife, unless she has been unfaithful, causes her to commit adultery. And anyone who marries a divorced woman also commits adultery.

## Teaching about Vows

"You have also heard that our ancestors were told, 'You must not break your vows; you must carry out the vows you make to the LORD.' But I say, do not make any vows! Do not say, 'By heaven!' because heaven is God's throne. And do not say, 'By the earth!' because the earth is his footstool. And do not say, 'By Jerusalem!' for Jerusalem is the city of the great King. Do not even say, 'By my head!' for you can't turn one hair white or black. Just say a simple, 'Yes, I will,' or 'No, I won't.' Anything beyond this is from the evil one.

## Teaching about Revenge

"You have heard the law that says the punishment must match the injury: 'An eye for an eye, and a tooth for a tooth.'

But I say, do not resist an evil person! If someone slaps you on the right cheek, offer the other cheek also. If you are sued in court and your shirt is taken from you, give your coat, too. If a soldier demands that you carry his gear for a mile, carry it two miles. Give to those who ask, and don't turn away from those who want to borrow.

## Teaching about Love for Enemies

"You have heard the law that says, 'Love your neighbor' and hate your enemy. But I say, love your enemies! Pray for those who persecute you! In that way, you will be acting as true children of your Father in heaven. For he gives his sunlight to both the evil and the good, and he sends rain on the just and the unjust alike. If you love only those who love you, what reward is there for that? Even corrupt tax collectors do that much. If you are kind only to your friends, how are you different than anyone else? Even pagans do that. But you are to be perfect, even as your Father in heaven is perfect.

## Teaching about Giving to the Needy

"Watch out! Don't do your good deeds publicly, to be admired by others, for you will lose the reward from your Father in heaven. When you give to someone in need, don't do as the hypocrites do—blowing trumpets in the synagogues and streets to call attention to their acts of charity! I tell you the truth, they have received all the reward they will ever get. But when you give to someone in need, don't let your left hand know what your right hand is doing. Give your gifts in private, and your Father, who sees everything, will reward you.

## Teaching about Prayer and Fasting

"When you pray, don't be like the hypocrites who love to pray publicly on street corners and in the synagogues where everyone can see them. I tell you the truth, that is all the reward they will ever get. But when you pray, go away by yourself, shut the door behind you, and pray to your Father in private. Then your Father, who sees everything, will reward you.

"When you pray, don't babble on and on as the Gentiles do. They think their prayers are answered merely by repeating their words again and again. Don't be like them, for your Father knows exactly what you need even before you ask him! Pray like this:

> "Our Father in heaven, may your name be kept
>      holy.
> May your kingdom come soon.
> May your will be done on earth, as it is in heaven.
> Give us today the food we need,
> and forgive us our sins, as we have forgiven
>      those who sin against us.
> And don't let us yield to temptation, but rescue
>      us from the evil one.

"If you forgive those who sin against you, your heavenly Father will forgive you. But if you refuse to forgive others, your Father will not forgive your sins.

"And when you fast, don't make it obvious, as the hypocrites do, for they try to look miserable and disheveled so people will admire them for their fasting. I tell you the truth that is the only reward they will ever get. But when you fast, comb your hair and wash your face. Then no one will notice that you are fasting, except your Father, who knows what you do in private. And your Father, who sees everything, will reward you.

## Teaching about Money and Possessions

"Don't store up treasures here on earth, where moths eat them and rust destroys them, and where thieves break in and steal. Store your treasures in heaven, where moths and rust cannot destroy, and thieves do not break in and steal. Wherever your treasure is, there the desires of your heart will also be.

"Your eye is a lamp that provides light for your body. When your eye is healthy, your whole body is filled with light. But when your eye is unhealthy, your whole body is filled with darkness. And if the light you think you have is actually darkness, how deep that darkness is!

"No one can serve two masters. For you will hate one and love the other; you will be devoted to one and despise the other. You cannot serve God and be enslaved to money.

"That is why I tell you not to worry about everyday life—whether you have enough food and drink, or enough clothes to wear. Isn't life more than food, and your body more than clothing? Look at the birds. They don't plant or harvest or store food in barns, for your heavenly Father feeds them. And aren't you far more valuable to him than they are? Can all your worries add a single moment to your life?

"And why worry about your clothing? Look at the lilies of the field and how they grow. They don't work or make their clothing, yet Solomon in all his glory was not dressed as beautifully as they are. And if God cares so wonderfully for wildflowers that are here today and thrown into the fire tomorrow, he will certainly care for you. Why do you have so little faith?

"So don't worry about these things, saying, 'What will we eat? What will we drink? What will we wear?' These things dominate the thoughts of unbelievers, but your heavenly Father already knows all your needs. Seek the Kingdom of God above all else, and live righteously, and he will give you everything you need.

"So don't worry about tomorrow, for tomorrow will bring its own worries. Today's trouble is enough for today.

## Do Not Judge Others

"Do not judge others, and you will not be judged. For you will be treated as you treat others. The standard you use in judging is the standard by which you will be judged.

"And why worry about a speck in your friend's eye when you have a log in your own? How can you think of saying to your friend, 'Let me help you get rid of that speck in your eye,' when you can't see past the log in your own eye? Hypocrite! First get rid of the log in your own eye; then you will see well enough to deal with the speck in your friend's eye.

"Don't waste what is holy on people who are unholy. Don't throw your pearls to pigs! They will trample the pearls, then turn and attack you.

## Effective Prayer

"Keep on asking, and you will receive what you ask for. Keep on seeking, and you will find. Keep on knocking, and the door will be opened to you. For everyone who asks, receives. Everyone who seeks, finds. And to everyone who knocks, the door will be opened.

"You parents—if your children ask for a loaf of bread, do you give them a stone instead? Or if they ask for a fish, do you give them a snake? Of course not! So if you sinful people know how to give good gifts to your children, how much more will your heavenly Father give good gifts to those who ask him.

## The Golden Rule

"Do to others whatever you would like them to do to you. This is the essence of all that is taught in the law and the prophets.

## The Narrow Gate

"You can enter God's Kingdom only through the narrow gate. The highway to hell is broad, and its gate is wide for the many who choose that way. But the gateway to life is very narrow and the road is difficult, and only a few ever find it.

## The Tree and Its Fruit

"Beware of false prophets who come disguised as harmless sheep but are really vicious wolves. You can identify them by their fruit, that is, by the way they act. Can you pick grapes from thornbushes, or figs from thistles? A good tree produces good fruit, and a bad tree produces bad fruit. A good tree can't produce bad fruit, and a bad tree can't produce good fruit. So every tree that does not produce good fruit is chopped down and thrown into the fire. Yes, just as you can identify a tree by its fruit, so you can identify people by their actions.

## True Disciples

"Not everyone who calls out to me, 'Lord! Lord!' will enter the Kingdom of Heaven. Only those who actually do the will of my Father in heaven will enter. On judgment day many will say to me, 'Lord! Lord! We prophesied in your name and cast out demons in your name and performed many miracles in your name.' But I will reply, 'I never knew you. Get away from me, you who break God's laws.'

## Building on a Solid Foundation

"Anyone who listens to my teaching follows it is wise, like a person who builds a house on solid rock. Though the rain comes in torrents and the floodwaters rise and the winds beat against that house, it won't collapse because it is built on bedrock. But anyone who hears my teaching and doesn't obey it is foolish, like a person who builds a house on sand. When the rains and floods come and the winds beat against that house, it will collapse with a mighty crash."

When Jesus had finished saying these things the crowds were amazed at his teaching, for he taught with real authority—quite unlike their teachers of religious law. (Matthew 5:1—7:29)

# APPENDIX TWO

"That is why I tell you not to worry about everyday life—whether you have enough food and drink, or enough clothes to wear. Isn't life more than food, and your body more than clothing? Look at the birds. They don't plant or harvest or store food in barns, for your heavenly Father feeds them. And aren't you far more valuable to him than they are? Can all your worries add a single moment to your life?

"And why worry about your clothing? Look at the lilies of the field and how they grow. They don't work or make their clothing, yet Solomon in all his glory was not dressed as beautifully as they are. And if God cares so wonderfully for wildflowers that are here today and thrown into the fire tomorrow, he will certainly care for you. Why do you have so little faith?

"So don't worry about these things, saying 'What will we eat? What will we drink? What will we wear?' These things dominate the thoughts of unbelievers, but your heavenly Father already knows all your needs. Seek the Kingdom of God above all else, and live righteously, and he will give you everything you need." (Matthew 6:25–33).

# APPENDIX THREE

The Jewish leaders began harassing Jesus for breaking the Sabbath rules. But Jesus replied, "My Father is always working, and so am I." So the Jewish leaders tried all the harder to find a way to kill him. For he not only broke the Sabbath, he called God his Father, thereby making himself equal with God.

So Jesus explained, "I tell you the truth, the Son can do nothing by himself. He does only what he sees the Father doing. Whatever the Father does, the Son also does. For the Father loves the Son and shows him everything he is doing. In fact, the Father will show him how to do even greater works than healing this man. Then you will truly be astonished. For just as the Father gives life to those he raises from the dead, so the Son gives life to anyone he wants. In addition, the Father judges no one. Instead, he has given the Son absolute authority to judge, so that everyone will honor the Son, just as they honor the Father. Anyone who does not honor the Son is certainly not honoring the Father who sent him.

"I tell you the truth, those who listen to my message and believe in God who sent me have eternal life. They will never be condemned for their sins, but they have already passed from death into life.

"And I assure you that the time is coming, indeed it's here now, when the dead will hear my voice—the voice of the Son of God. And those who listen will live. The Father has life in himself, and he has granted that same life-giving power to his Son. And he has given him authority to judge everyone because he is the Son of Man. Don't be so surprised! Indeed, the time is coming when all the dead in their graves will hear the voice of God's Son, and they will rise again. Those who have done good will rise to experience eternal life, and those who have continued in evil will rise to experience judgment. I can do nothing on my own. I judge as God tells me. Therefore, my judgment is just, because I carry out the will of the one who sent me, not my own will." (John 5:16–30)

# NOTES

1   Jimmy Carter, *A Call to Action* (New York, NY: Simon & Schuster, 2014), 1–2.

2   Joseph Ellis, *The Quartet* (New York, NY: Alfred A. Knopf, 2015), xii.

3   Ibid., 9.

4   Ibid., xix.

5   Ibid., 10.

6   Ibid.

7   Ibid., 15.

8   Ibid., 76.

9   Ibid., 98.

10   Ibid., 99.

11   Ibid., 103.

12   Ibid., 104.

13   Ibid., 126–127.

14   Ibid., 139.

15   Ibid., 136–137.

16   Ibid., 141.

17   Ibid., 143.

18   Ibid., 144–145.

19   Ibid., 151.

20   Linda Hirshman, *Sisters in Law* (New York, NY: HarperCollins, 2015), 38.

21   Sue Poorman Richards and Lawrence O. Richards, *Women of the Bible* (Nashville, TN: Thomas Nelson, 2003), 91.

22   Scot McKnight, *The Blue Parakeet* (Grand Rapids, MI: Zondervan, 2008), 174.

23   J. Lee Grady, *10 Lies the Church Tells Women* (Lake Mary, FL: Charisma House, 2000), 166.

24   Ibid., 166–67.

25   Scot McKnight, *The Blue Parakeet* (Grand Rapids, MI: Zondervan, 2008), 143.

26   Sarah Sumner, *Men and Women in the Church* (Downers Grove, IL: InterVarsity Press, 2003), 125.

27   Sue Poorman Richards and Lawrence O. Richards, *Women of the Bible* (Nashville, TN: Thomas Nelson, 2003), 252–53.

28   John Temple Bristow, *What Paul Really Said about Women* (New York, NY: HarperCollins Publishers, 1988), 31.

29   Sue Poorman Richards and Lawrence O. Richards, *Women of the Bible* (Nashville, TN: Thomas Nelson, 2003), 158–59.

30   J. Lee Grady, *10 Lies the Church Tells Women* (Lake Mary, FL: Charisma House, 2000), 123.

31   John Temple Bristow, *What Paul Really Said about Women* (New York, NY: HarperCollins Publishers, 1988), 5.

32   Ibid., 6.

33   Ibid., 6

34   Ibid., 33.

35   Ibid., xi–xii.

36   Ibid., 35–38.

37   Gilbert Bilezikian, *Beyond Sex Roles* (Grand Rapids, MI: Baker Academic, 2006), 120.

38 Sarah Sumner, *Men and Women in the Church* (Downers Grove, IL: InterVarsity Press, 2003), 212–13.

39 J. Lee Grady, *10 Lies the Church Tells Women* (Lake Mary, FL: Charisma House, 2000), 62.

40 John Temple Bristow, *What Paul Really Said about Women* (New York, NY: HarperCollins Publishers, 1988), 62–63.

41 Ibid., 63.

42 J. Lee Grady, *10 Lies the Church Tells Women* (Lake Mary, FL: Charisma House, 2000), 68–69.

43 Ibid., 65–66.

44 Gilbert Bilezikian, *Beyond Sex Roles* (Grand Rapids, MI: Baker Academic, 2006), 137.

45 John Temple Bristow, *What Paul Really Said about Women* (New York, NY: HarperCollins Publishers, 1988), 72.

46 Ibid., 71.

47 Ibid., 71.

48 Ibid., 29.

49 Rick Warren, *The Purpose Driven Life* (Grand Rapids, MI: Zondervan, 2002, 2011, 2012), 76.

50 Joyce Meyer, *A Leader in the Making* (New York, NY: Warner Books, 2001), 141.

51 Rick Warren, *The Purpose Driven Life* (Grand Rapids, MI: Zondervan, 2002, 2011, 2012), 36.

52 Bill Hybels, *Courageous Leadership*, (Grand Rapids, Michigan: Zondervan, 2002), 32.

53 Linda Hirshman, *Sisters in Law* (New York, NY: HarperCollins, 2015), xvii.

54   Ibid., 36.

55   Ibid., 24.

56   Ibid., xvi.

57   Ibid., 25.

58   Ibid., 28.

59   Ibid., 26.

60   Ibid., 27.

61   Ibid., 40.

62   Ibid., 123.

63   Ibid., 101.

64   Ibid., 104.

65   Ibid., 170.

66   Ibid., 171.

67   Ibid., 171–72.

68   Ibid., 172.

69   Ibid., 173.

70   Ibid., 164.

71   Ibid., 166.

72   Ibid., 216.

73   Ibid., 217.

74   Ibid.

75   Ibid., 219–20.

76   Ibid., 221.

77   Ibid., 234.

78   Ibid., 237.

79   Ibid., 243.

80   Ibid., 248.

81   Ibid., 249.

82   Ibid., 264.

83   Ibid., 252–53.

84  Ibid., 265–66.

85  Ibid., 266.

86  Ibid., 273.

87  Ibid., 282.

88  Ibid., 285.

89  Ibid., 287.

90  Ibid., 291.

91  Sarah Sumner, *Men and Women in the Church* (Downers Grove, IL: InterVarsity Press, 2003), 26–27.

92  C. Bernard Ruffin, *The Twelve: The Lives of the Apostles after Calvary* (Huntington, IN: Our Sunday Visitor, 1997, 1994), 33.

93  Ibid., 50–54.

94  William Steuart McBirnie, *The Search for the Twelve Apostles* (Wheaton, IL: Tyndale House Publishers, 1973), 65–66.

95  Bruce Wilkinson, *Secrets of the Vine* (Sisters, OR: Multnomah Publishers, Inc., 2001), 117–18.

96  Gary Thomas, *Sacred Pathways* (Grand Rapids, MI: Zondervan Publishing House, 2000), 21.

97  Ibid., 18.

98  Ibid., 23.

99  Ibid., 26.

100  Ibid., 117.

101  Ibid.

102  Ibid., 126.

103  Ibid., 118.